MAN HANDLING

How To Handle
Any Man,
Any Time

Susan Thomas

Copyright 1994, Susan Thomas. All rights reserved.

Written permission must be received from the publisher before using or reproducing any portion of this book, other than for the purpose of critical reviews or articles.

Director of Photography:
Bill Thorup
X-Press Studio
Nashville, Tennessee

Edited by:
Richard Courtney and Maryglenn McCombs

Design, typography, and text production:
Maryglenn McCombs

Cover design and production:
Susan McGlohon
The Pure Idea Workshop
Nashville, Tennessee

Front cover photography:
Bill Thorup
X-Press Studio
Nashville, Tennessee

Back cover photography:
Dean Dixon
Dean Dixon Photography
Nashville, Tennessee

Security by Bogart McCloud

For interviews and other information:
Southern Publishers Group
Birmingham, Alabama
1-800-628-0903

ISBN: 0-9635026-8-9

Library of Congress Catalog Card Number: 072722

Eggman Publishing
2909 Poston Avenue
Suite 203
Nashville, TN 37203
(615) 327-9390

Merry Christmas Andria,

I love you more than I could ever express in words. May your dreams come true in 2001.

To Coyote McCloud,
The Ultimate
Man Handling
Challenge

Love Always,

Michael

INTRODUCTION

The phone rang at 2:23 AM.

"I've got to talk to you!" gasped my friend Donna.

"What's the matter?" I mumbled drowsily. "Are you okay?"

"You are not going to believe what he did this time! He called at seven and we were supposed to ..."

I listened.

She ranted.

I yawned.

She sniffled.

I snored and she yelled at me for not helping her decide what to do about *him* this time.

"Listen to me!" I snapped.

"YOU are the problem, not him!

"YOU have let him treat you like this!

"Do YOU hear me?"

There was a sulking silence.

"I swear," I continued, "one of these days I'm going to write a book on how to handle any man, any time, so you'll quit calling me in the middle of the night!"

"Fine!" she screamed back. "I'll buy the damn book!"

Click.

She hung up on me.

Being best friends, all was well by morning.

But, before another full moon could come around, Donna was back on the phone at midnight, with yet another male dilemma.

I began thinking — and, being a newspaper reporter, I began asking questions.

It started with a few friends and then spread to a few acquaintances. Soon, I was calling friends of friends who were willing to tell me how they had successfully dealt with particular types of men.

The pattern emerged quickly.

Every man falls into a certain category. Given the time of day or the weather, he might stray a bit from his pattern, but it doesn't happen often. In large part, men stick to their type and share similar traits. They share similar likes and dislikes. They also share dreams of their ideal woman.

This commonality is the reason men are predictable. The only trick is figuring out which man type you have set your eyes on *before* you proceed.

Man Handling profiles eighteen types of men, offers a real-life situation showing how a woman has successfully dealt with the individual male type to find happiness — with or without them. It then offers explanations of how to handle these very different male types, along with simplified tips to remember.

So, Donna, it's almost midnight. Turn the page.

CONTENTS

I   Mr. Animal-Attraction   1
Just like in the movies, you catch his eye across a crowded room. Your heart starts pumping fast, but you know that love is not causing this reaction. How to handle the lust.

II   Mr. Homecoming-King   7
When the guy you swooned over at the prom twenty years ago reappears in your life, what do you do — stare at his beer belly or re-love him? How to handle his re-entry.

III   Mr. Paranoia-Strikes-Deep   13
He is so into himself you are often tempted to put him out of his misery. How to keep from laughing in his face as you try to find out if there is any hope for him at all.

IV   Mr. Catch-Me-If-You-Can   19
This Peter Pan will never grow up and you will be fooling yourself if you think you can snare him with a hook. He will always be searching for Never-Never Land. Do you want to be his Wendy?

V   Mr. Steady-As-You-Go   25
You can win a lot and lose little if you tie up with the guy who every girl's parents adored in high school. Can you shift into low gear and glide? How to trade the glitter for the gold.

VI   Mr. Born-To-The-Wild   31
From mountain climbers to fishermen, you will have trouble keeping this man out of the wild, so do not bother trying. The good news is that it can get pretty wild in a tent.

VII   Mr. Don't-Miss-Your-Chance   37
It's best to make sure you know what you are getting into before you climb into the Rolls. He is the man who always wants the woman he cannot get. How to be his elusive catch, time and time again.

VIII   Mr. Hello-In-There   43
He talks tough. But what is that you see deep in his eyes — alone or lonely? How to be patient enough to find out what is keeping him hostage inside. Will he ever come out to play?

IX   Mr. Can-We-Say-Ma-Ma?   49
Younger men have such an innocent sweetness about them. They can be addictive. But, have you looked in the mirror lately? How to take the compliment without breaking the law.

X   Mr. Mentor-Me-Too   53
Yes, he's helped you. Yes, you appreciate it. But, are you going to sleep with him? How to handle the morning after, or the years ahead, whether your answer is yes, no, or maybe later.

XI   Mr. I'm-Too-Sexy-For-My-Socks   59
Sometimes men are simply too good-looking for their own good. Can you be the one to show him real life is more than skin deep? How to negate all those years of "Mirror, Mirror on the Wall."

XII   Mr. Forget-Me-Not   63
Being absent-minded was kind of cute at first. But forgetting your anniversary was rough. Missing your birthday was enough. How to give him a memory or show him the door.

XIII   Mr. President   69
When it comes to material possessions or you, the Jaguar and his job take first and second place. How to be happy in third place or make a place of your own in this man's life.

XIV   Mr. Roll-With-The-Dice   75
The soul of a risk-taker can never be tamed, but it can be handled. The trick comes from within you, not him. Are you ready for a ride on the roulette table? How to win the bet with this man.

XV   Mr. Save-The-Snails   81
You may be an endangered species if you do not know how to handle this crusader. He has a heart like Noah's, and you cannot fight his instincts. How to be his partner in the world he wants to save.

XVI   Mr. Not-In-This-Lifetime   85
There is no place, whatsoever, in any woman's life for this man. He is an abuser, plain and simple. How to recognize these spineless creatures, get out quick, and never look back.

XVII   Mr. Dream-A-Little-Dream-With-Me   91
A man with a gypsy soul always follows the beat of a different drummer. How to tap your foot to his tune or leave him while you're both still smiling.

XVIII   Mr. Take-Two   97
His bedside manner is magnificent, but you don't seem to exist outside the bed sheets. How to break into his mind and make him take notice, even with your clothes on.

The Ten Commandments of Man Handling

For every type of man, there are incalculable ways for a woman to go about handling them. Overall, there are certain tenets every woman must follow, not necessarily for a man, but for herself. No matter what man your loves fall upon, remember these ten tips, above all:

1. Believe in yourself.
2. Know when to run.
3. Never cling.
4. Think before you react.
5. Keep taxi fare.
6. Stand your ground.
7. Make no ultimatums.
8. Never whine.
9. Shut up before you lie.
10. Give it your best shot.

CHAPTER I

Mr. Animal Attraction

Traits: Sexy
Physical
Intriguing

Likes: Sex
Secrets
Playing

Dislikes: Responsibility
Seriousness
Confinement

His Ideal Woman: Sexy
Sensual
Imaginative

HIS PROFILE

While they rarely tell a soul, virtually every woman past puberty — no matter what her age, social status, personality or morals — will stumble upon this man at least once in her lifetime.

He will appear from nowhere, perhaps a co-worker in a different department, a long-lost acquaintance, a friend of a friend, or face in the crowd. But the moment her eyes meet his, the rest is fairly predictable. What usually follows is a hot round of primitive animal attraction.

When this initial attraction strikes a woman, she must make an instant decision: should I stay, or run away? Either way, there's an excellent chance that initial jolt of animal magnetism may never leave her memory.

To make things difficult, there is no way to forecast when or where this man may appear.

Nor is there a way to pinpoint what form this man may take in physical shape, size or looks, mental ability, profession, finances — absolutely nothing. His appeal is wholly irrational, completely left up to the imagination of the woman.

Once the initial sparks have flared, very few, if any woman ever considers a long-term future with this man. Instead, most women instinctively recognize this as a one-time opportunity to throw worry out the window and mindlessly attack this animal of passion — at least once.

MAGGIE'S STORY

"Even though I had seen him before, the night I *really* saw him, I was horribly depressed," said Maggie, 41, a hair stylist in New Orleans.

"My mother had been seriously ill. I was in a rut at my job, my birthdays seemed to be coming every month making me older and older, and the guy I had been living with for three years didn't seem to understand why I wasn't my usual old self. I loved him, and he loved me, but couldn't explain why I was down.

"One Friday night, a couple of girls at work and I had rented a limousine to take a friend out on a girls-only party before her wedding the next day. We had a great time, bar-hopping down on Bourbon Street after dinner. We ended up at a small corner bar that was nothing more than a bar and a couple of pool tables.

"I was playing pool with one of my friends when *he* walked in. I recognized him from the gym and remembered having talked to him a couple of times. I knew that he was an engineer of some kind, but that was about it.

"After my friend scratched on the eight-ball, the only shot she'd made, he walked over and asked to play. I told him he could and admitted that I had forgotten his name.

"Phil," he said.

Maggie said that other than the usual pool-playing banter, she paid very little attention to him until she accidentally backed into him after making a great shot.

"I turned my head over my shoulder to say 'sorry,' and it was as if I was seeing him for the first time. It was his eyes that got me. He didn't look like a movie star and wasn't even that well-built. But there was something intense in his eyes.

"Words don't seem to describe it. It was purely electric sex appeal. I wanted him. *Bad.*

"It was crazy, but even though neither one of us said anything, I knew the feeling was mutual. I hardly knew this guy, but it was agonizing to leave that place when my friends were ready to go.

"It only got worse when I got home. I fought a restless battle with my pillow all night. My boyfriend, sensing my tension, asked me what was wrong. Of course there wasn't anything I could say to him, so I just laid there in the dark with my eyes wide open replaying that instant when I brushed into Phil and saw that look in his eyes."

With no sleep, Maggie headed straight for the gym the following morning.

"I would like to be able to say I was confused, but I wasn't," she explained. "I didn't want him to ask me out to dinner. I didn't want to have long discussions of where he came from or where I was at that point in my life. I just wanted to touch him and for him to touch me. That was it.

"The thought never occurred that he might not be there. I knew he would be there, and he was. I wasted no time. I started some silly small talk as we jogged around the track. We may have made it around three times. Then we left for his place.

"He was a bachelor for sure. The place was nice, but he walked in first, pushing dirty dishes in the sink and throwing dirty clothes in the closet. I sat down on the couch. He brought bottled water with two wine glasses and proposed we have a toast to my friend who was getting married that afternoon.

"It was goofy, but fun, and I was as light-headed from having no sleep as I was from sitting there with him.

"We just stared at each other. I told him I had no earthly idea why I was there, that I was happy in a relationship and didn't want to jeopardize that. Then I admitted I had been feeling down lately, and it felt good to be with someone I didn't have to worry about or impress.

"There was a long pause before he smiled. I leaned over a gave him a light kiss on the lips. He still didn't say anything, so I came out with that pitiful question, 'What are you thinking about?'

"He said, 'I'm just wondering if you're going to kiss me again.'

"A second later, I was all over him.

"Two hours later, in a sweaty heap, we had done just about everything this side of intercourse. At that moment, I wanted that badly, but something stopped me from going all the way.

"I was totally exhausted. I got up, pulled on my clothes and he walked me to the door. Then he kissed me on the forehead, and I left. No guilt — no nothing that I would have expected to feel. I just had this good feeling for days, and I can still feel a little tingle even now when I think about that sexy, secret night and day."

HOW TO HANDLE THIS MAN

First of all, if you have had an encounter or two with this animal of your attraction, do not put yourself down.

It happens. The fact is that it usually happens when women are in some kind of emotional turmoil, for any number of reasons. It has much more to do with trying to escape from whatever curves life has thrown your way, than it reflects any lapse of morality, religion, or individual beliefs.

In Maggie's case, her mind needed a diversion as much as or perhaps more than her body needed physical contact with Phil. Luckily for her, she was smart enough to choose a man who held at least a fleeting genuine affection for her, and more importantly, she chose a man who accepted the ground rules — a few hours together and then a goodbye.

In the weeks and months which passed after Maggie's moment of animal attraction, daydreams of Phil actually helped pull her out of her depression. These were not dreams of a life with Phil, merely memories of their moments together. That helped Maggie balance her concerns about her mother's health, realize that she was still attractive despite the passing years and, just as importantly, renewed her commitment to the man she truly loved.

But, be warned. Giving in to animal attraction can be a dangerous game. You risk losing someone you love. Without proper protection, you could risk contracting anything from herpes to HIV. If you fail to match up with a man responsible enough to play by the ground rules, you could end up stalked by an animal who is hard to lose.

The best advice is simple: be smart.

Animal attraction is a risky business. If you are a woman who eventually has to "tell-all," *don't even try it.*

MAN HANDLING TIPS

1. First and foremost, remember safe sex.

2. You are human. Things happen. Trash the guilt.

3. Keep the memory for your days in a rocking chair.

CHAPTER II

Mr. Homecoming King

Traits: Stable
Predictable
Disenchanted

Likes: The Old Days
TV Sports
Their Kids

Dislikes: Growing Old
Regrets
What Could Have Been

His Ideal Woman: Homecoming Queen
Faithful
Ego Builder

HIS PROFILE

You will remember him amidst the pom-poms and confetti.

The president of the senior class. The captain of the football team. You would have paid him to let you carry his books to class.

He was the hero of your high school world, which at the time, was your whole world.

There was no way to predict that once the high school commencement was over, each and every one of your classmates would scatter with and against the wind, never again to come together in full to create that small society everyone remembers as "the senior class."

Sad? Yes, but not really. Reality? Yes, but not sad.

For anyone more than five years past high school graduation, it is easy to see that the high school fish bowl in which we all once swam was indeed very small, limiting our visions of the wide world lurking in waiting outside our front doors.

For some, however, those big fish from those little bowls return, and the task is confronting what you thought about them then and, more importantly, what you think of them now.

It is a tender game, one that should be as kind as possible, but at the same time as honest as possible.

High school illusions were and are no more than that — illusions.

What happens when that old hero shows up in your life today?

JEANNIE'S STORY

"I will take to task any woman, or any man, who says she or he didn't have a love in high school," said Jeannie, 38, a costume designer in Los Angeles.

"That is not to say it was physically consummated or serious. Simply stated, everyone knew someone in high school that, at least for some time in space, they thought they loved.

"It somehow happens when you toss a bunch of people into a confined environment and force them find their own way.

"My high school love was a boy named Sam, the captain of the football team. At that point in my life, he had everything. He was popular, cute, and every other girl in school wanted him.

"What more could I want?"

Almost twenty years passed between high school graduation and the night Jeannie and Sam met again. Jeannie had been married and divorced once and had a daughter in college. He was twice divorced and had a teenage son and daughter who lived with his ex-wife.

"It was an aimless night," Jeannie said. "My best girlfriend, who went to school with Sam and me, stopped by my house on her way home from work because neither of us had a date or anything else better to do.

"She and I started talking, and within a few minutes, Sam's name came up. Neither of us had any idea if he was still in town, if he was married, or anything. Before I realized what she was doing, my friend picked up the phone and called his mother, who we had both known from way back when.

"With the phone to her ear, I felt a really strange sensation when she yelled out Sam's name. Apparently he had stopped by his mother's on his way home and had answered the phone.

"Before I had a chance to react, my friend invited him to stop by for a drink and visit with us after all these years. When she hung up the phone, I couldn't decide whether to kill her or kiss her. I was completely on edge. I went to my room and put on a little makeup and fixed my hair. Suddenly, I was reminded of the way I used to primp for hours before Sam came over to pick me up.

"We were sitting at my kitchen table when the doorbell rang. I made her go to the door.

"He took a long look at me and said, 'You haven't changed a bit.'

"Knowing I was two dress sizes larger, knowing I had wrinkles around my eyes, his words made me feel like all those years had magically disappeared without a trace.

"When Sam sat down at the table, we were looking at each other so intently that my girlfriend took the hint and went home.

"After she left, Sam and I talked."

Jeannie said that in between their words, she noticed his stomach pouch that had not been there the night he caught the winning touchdown pass at Homecoming. She noticed the silver hairs that had begun to highlight his dark black hair. She also heard the sound of his voice that seemed much more down to earth than the voice she remembered telling her that he was out to conquer the world.

As she listened, she said she could not help but open herself up for comparison, at least in her mind.

Her stomach was nowhere near as flat as it was the last time she had seen him. Her hair was a little too red, thanks to the last color she had gotten at the salon. And, as she listened as he spoke, she realized she, too, was no longer the young high school kid they once had both been.

"We walked into the living room on his way out, and he kissed me," she says. "My head was spinning, remembering how I felt at seventeen when he first kissed me, but still trying to make sense of him kissing me twenty years later. It was strange.

"I didn't know what to say when he asked me out.

"Feebly, I muttered 'Sure' and told him to give me a call."

HOW TO HANDLE THIS MAN

Are you happy to see him again or just desperate for a man? Either way, you have to lock into *today* — the real place and the real time.

Too often, when old boyfriends come back, it is easy to slip into that retrospective of "when," even though that "when" has been gone as long as curfews and your mother telling you to "sit like a lady."

The toughest part of handling this man is coming to grips with the years that have passed in your own lives.

There is no doctrine that says he is any

better or worse than when you knew him then. The growing up changes you have gone through will determine whether you are following a butterfly of today or one that flew away years ago.

The best way to handle this man is to give it a chance.

Listen. Talk. Reminisce. Most importantly, share your dreams of the future to see if any of them mesh. Who, what, and where do you both want to be ten years from now, just in time for the 30th year class reunion?

Remember that with this man, you have everything to gain yet little to lose. Whatever you may have lost with him a long time ago is history.

Today is what matters.

MAN HANDLING TIPS

1. Don't judge him by who he was.

2. Remember that you aren't the same either.

3. Change is the only constant in life.

CHAPTER III
Mr. Paranoia-Strikes-Deep

Traits: Fanatical
Detached
Brooding

Likes: Anxiety
Arguments
Chaos

Dislikes: Success
Praise
Comparisons

His Ideal Woman: Tenacious
Intuitive
Maternal

HIS PROFILE

This guy is one piece of work.

On first glance, you immediately know that it took him longer to choose his outfit than it took you to call your mother, feed the dog, shower, dry your hair, put on your make-up, dress and leave a long note for your roommate.

Even as potent as the word paranoid is, it fails miserably in its attempt to describe this man. He is meticulous about everything, from each strand of his hair to the tips of his twice-shined shoes. He has the power to bring out your primitive urge to accidently spill a glass of water on him to see if he will freak out.

Reason denies you the ability to do that, but this man has the potential to drive you absolutely nuts. The reason he survives with women is because the root of his paranoia is insecurity. He feels he will never be completely accepted by anyone for anything.

How did he get this way? That is anybody's guess, but the most common reason is a mother who never quite thought her son lived up to her expectations — and told him so repeatedly.

VERONICA'S STORY

"I really needed a date," says Veronica, 40, a free-lance writer from Detroit. "I had recently divorced for the second time. I had no children and it seemed like every man I met was married.

"When I ran into Ronald in the bookstore, in the Self-Help section, no less, I thought he was cute. I could tell he was a couple of years older than I was, and he was not wearing a wedding band, which automatically piqued my interest.

"But, he was weird from the start. After we talked a while, I gave him my phone number — and he gave me his.

"I waited two weeks to see if he would call. Not a chance. I grew tired of waiting, had a couple of drinks one Friday night, picked up the phone and called him. Surprisingly, he was quite nice. He seemed thrilled that I had called. With nothing to lose, I invited him to join me for a drink with a couple of my friends the next night.

"You would have thought I had asked him to marry me! He stuttered and stammered around and finally said something like, 'I'd like to meet you, but I'm not up to meeting your friends yet.'

"Stunned by his reaction, I quickly asked him to join me for a drink before I met my friends, to which he agreed.

"Every time I think about that first night I want to laugh! When I got to the club where we had agreed to meet, the only place to sit down was a table for four in the bar. I was sitting there alone when Ronald walked in. He looked great and gave me a smile as he walked over and sat down. But before I could say hello, he looked across the table at the chair on the other side of me, jumped up and said, 'Oh, would you rather me sit over here?'

"I didn't know what to say. As if it made any difference which chair he sat in!

"That is only one of a thousand examples of how even the most simple things were a big deal to Ronald."

In fairness to Ronald, Veronica says he settled down considerably after they started dating.

"The problem was that I really liked him, but the things he did drove me crazy," she says. "For example, if we went out and came back to my place, the first thing he would do was call his house to see who had called him on his answering machine. To my recollection, there were never any important or urgent calls, but that didn't stop him from worrying that there might be.

"Another example. One night he brought Chinese food to my house. I was not very hungry that night, so I put mine in the refrigerator. The next morning, as he was walking out the kitchen door, he actually retrieved my dinner from the refrigerator and said, 'I'll take this for my lunch.'

"He was always thinking about himself — and no one else."

The real problem in their relationship, however, soon appeared.

"Jealousy," Veronica says flatly. "He was undoubtedly the most jealous person I ever knew existed. He became furious if a man looked at me. He became upset if I said hello to another man. He became angry if I talked to the mailman too long. It was crazy. He was never mean to me, but he would get red in the face and sulk.

"After three months, I had had it. The paranoia, let alone his jealousy, was not worth it. I finally had to tell him to get lost."

HOW TO HANDLE THIS MAN

Throwing this man away, although often the most viable option, is perhaps too easy. After all, it is the only way to validate his paranoid belief that you will one day, anyway.

If you have the patience, slow down before you throw.

In a world where so many men have enormously inflated egos, it can be refreshing to meet a man who does not trust any move he makes.

Imagine what demons must be inhabiting his mind to make him so insecure. They cannot be pleasant, and chances are he would give anything to find a woman who could help him sort out his distrust and distaste for himself.

What, then, does it take to effectively handle this man? The answer is a mother figure with an attitude. A woman strong enough to see through his fears, yet one who possesses the understanding to help him take a look from the outside inward in order to see if some minor readjustments in his mind's mirror might help him chill out.

It takes a gentle but firm hand on the part of the woman. At every crossroad — be it a jealous outburst or the hour it takes for him to choose his shirt or to take out the trash — this man must be confronted.

Why do you feel this way?

What can *we* do to save you all this useless turmoil?

How can *we* work through it so that this does not happen again?

Slow and steady is the only way to handle

this man if you have the patience to work with him.

Most women, like Veronica, choose to move on to more secure pastures.

"I still love Ronald to death," she says, "He's a sweetheart. I truly hope some woman will come along one day, sit him down and help him figure himself out."

MAN HANDLING TIPS

1. Try not to laugh in his face.

2. Understand his problems came along a long time before you did.

3. Tell him he needs to get a life, with or without you.

CHAPTER IV

Mr. Catch-Me-If-You-Can

Traits: Debonair
Introspective
Chameleon

Likes: Challenges
Compliments
Daydreaming

Dislikes: Status-Quo
Schedules
Tunnel Vision

His Ideal Woman: Physical
Flirtatious
Confident

HIS PROFILE

This man is always "on," be it in bed or in front of a crowd. He thrives on his internal wellspring of enthusiasm to conquer any endeavor that places him in the spotlight. He rises to any occasion, playing the role like a pro.

If he discovers your last boyfriend was a champ in bed, he will attempt to discover ways to raise the championship level so that you consider him the best. If he needs an increase in income to impress you, he will find a way to make the money. If he cares about you, he will read your mind, without your ever knowing it, and then do whatever is necessary to snare your heart.

Mr. Catch-Me-If-You-Can is extremely street-smart. His expert use of knowledge about people — and button pushing — can lure a woman into a blitz-like romance.

Behind his smile, this man is, for the most part, out for himself. His need for acceptance is so great that he hones his chameleon ways to endear himself however is necessary to reach his latest goal. Then, if his attention wanes, his soul goes searching for that next level of success, be it in his career or his love life.

SALLY'S STORY

"This sounds cliche, but Scott took my breath away the first moment I laid eyes on him," says Sally, 29, a Midwestern public relations agent. "It was instant intoxication."

At the time, Sally had been assigned to help coach Scott, one of the highest-profile male models in America, on how to conduct interviews after the release of his first book, a photo prospective on the behind-the- scenes life of male models.

"I went to New York to work with him for two weeks before his book signing tour began," Sally says. "I'd never met him before, never even seen a picture that I could match to his name, though I later discovered I'd seen his face for years, in ads in everything from *Gentlemen's Quarterly* to *Ladies Home Journal*.

"My job was to coach first-time authors, and I'll admit I was more than a little eager to coach Scott since my usually prim and proper boss had used the word 'hunk' to describe him. I was not dating anybody special at the time, so I thought the New York trip could be a lot of fun.

"My initial excitement was doused the day I arrived and called him to confirm our dinner, which had been planned for that night. He was pleasant, but told me vaguely that he could spare only about an hour early in the evening because of previous dinner plans.

"I assumed him to be a stuck-up, pretty boy with not much happening cerebrally."

Sally and Scott agreed that he would come to her hotel room about six o'clock to review the plan for the next two weeks.

"I don't consider myself a raving beauty by any means," says Sally, underestimating her chiseled cheekbones, long dark hair and sensuous demeanor. "But the sound of his voice on the phone let me know first hand that he was not exactly thrilled over the prospect of meeting some moppish P.R. agent from the Midwest.

"That infuriated me. I'm extremely proud of my work, I'm pretty damn good at it, and from what I'd heard about Scott's public speaking, he needed me. So what if I'm not model material? I don't look *that* bad.

"I decided to give it right back to him. I bought a new outfit — a plain but classy off-white crushed silk dress. I spent the afternoon taking a long bubble bath, doing my nails, twisting my hair halfway up in a windblown look, and experimenting with my make-up.

"At half past five, I called room service, ordered a good California Cabernet Sauvignon and relaxed.

"The phone rang right at six. He was in the lobby. I told him since he only had an hour, he might as well come up, shake hands, and hopefully schedule a meeting for the next day. I gave him the room number.

"He knocked. I opened the door and stuck out my hand. Then, we both froze. He was undoubtedly the best looking man I had ever seen in my entire life.

"But the best part about it was that he acting more nervous than me.

"'You — you're Sally?' he asked in a whisper.

His awkwardness steadied my resolve.

"Yes," I said, squarely, "won't you come in?"

He did, but stopped inside the door and

stared at me. When I offered him a glass of wine, all he could muster was a mumble.

"I asked coyly if something was wrong. He shook his head and stammered, 'Oh, no, I'm sorry. I just wasn't expecting you, I mean somebody like you. I mean, I guess I thought public relations flacks were, oh, how would I say, librarians or something?'

"I just smiled."

Two hours later, Sally and Scott were eating onion rings and ribs at Tony Roma's, following a discreet call he had made to cancel his "previous" dinner plans.

Two weeks later, Sally and Scott were a steady twosome when the time came for him to start his book tour and for her to return to Minneapolis.

"He had his publishing firm arrange for me to accompany him on the tour. This was the beginning of a relationship with a kind of man I had never known before.

"Everything had been great up to that point, but a little voice told me I was climbing out on a limb."

HOW TO HANDLE THIS MAN

This highly complex man is somewhat of a cross between Captain Hook and Peter Pan. Competitive to the core, he will never lose that gusto that has been building since his days as captain of the high school football team or some other conquest. No matter what age he attains, his youthful spirit will outshine any strands of gray hair.

It is his hybrid personality which makes this man one of the toughest of all men to handle.

First and foremost, a woman must understand that what she sees is not always what she gets. He is so adept at blending into any situation that she can easily slip into that no-woman's land of believing he is hooked, even after he has started looking around.

To be true, a woman who makes this man her own must be even smarter than he is, especially in intuitive, street-wise ways. She must be capable of listening, as well as observing his actions in order to head off a kiss-off which would blindside a less shrewd woman.

Unfortunately, that is exactly what happened to Sally.

After two fabulous weeks with Scott, she made the wrong decision when she agreed to accompany him on tour beyond the initial two week arrangement. In those first two weeks, Scott knew he truly needed her tutoring in order to excel on the book tour. Sally's nice looks and commanding behavior had been an added bonus.

But Sally's strongest asset — his need for her help so that he could do well on the tour — slipped away as he gained his own confidence in speaking to the crowds. An adept student, he had learned quickly. Having Sally around turned into a nuisance for two reasons: he no longer really needed her, and her own self-importance of being on the road with him diminished daily.

Sally soon found herself on the other end of the phone when he called at the last minute to cancel dinner because "something had come up." And she knew, without a doubt, that "something" was some cute young thing. Her self-esteem tumbled, as did the relationship.

"What should I have done?" Sally asked several months later.

Sad but true, she was on the right track the first day, and even during the two-weeks tutoring him. But deciding to go on tour with him, despite the high temptation, was a disaster. If she cared enough about Scott after those two weeks, she should have used this as a window of opportunity to set the stage to see if a deeper relationship may have grown.

First, she should have declined to go on his tour, letting him know her professional commitment was just as compelling and important as his, i.e., there was probably another good-looking man who needed her.

Second, with both on an even playing field, she would have been able to accept his invitations for special weekend rendezvous that he arranged, while he would have been able to meet her on special outings she arranged.

Third, and most importantly, she should have maintained her self-esteem and belief in herself at all costs. This Peter Pan man knows when he's found a Wendy, a woman with a will of her own with no strings attached.

MAN HANDLING TIPS

1. Make sure you're up for the challenge.

2. Keep your wits about you at all times.

3. Even if you love him, let him know you can make it without him.

CHAPTER V

Mr. Steady-As-You-Go

Traits: Dependable
Trustworthy
Gullible

Likes: TV
Backyard Basketball
Sunday Naps

Dislikes: Dressing Up
Social Scenes
Gossip

His Ideal Woman: Earthy
Stubborn
Fair

HIS PROFILE

He is the boy your parents approved of in high school. His word is written in stone. His actions are always that of a gentleman. He has never missed helping an elderly woman cross a street. And he would fight for the honor of any woman — whether a wife, lover, or friend.

Long ago, this man decided that life is best when it is safe and secure, even if that means foregoing climbing up a ladder toward a higher education or a treasure chest on a South Seas island. He is forever practical, helpful, dependable and down to earth. For these reasons, everyone — from old ladies to his boss — loves him. They simply cannot help it.

He is most comfortable at home with his family in a stable, predictable environment, whether it is a home with his mother or his wife.

On the other hand, he is ill at ease in social situations, often becoming tongue-tied and awkward. Far and away, his most attractive feature is his loving heart which he is ready to share anytime, any place with anyone.

AMANDA'S STORY

"I knew he was special from the moment I met Dale," says Amanda, 35, a free-lance writer from Atlanta. "We worked together and we got along great. Back then, the thought of a romantic relationship was out of the question because he had a steady girlfriend.

"I guess it was two years after he left town that I heard from him. He and his girlfriend had broken up, and he was coming through Atlanta on business. He asked if I wanted to go to a movie with him.

"I was tickled to death to hear from him. It had been years since any man had asked me to go to the movies on a first date. I felt like I was back in high school.

"I was thrilled because he wasn't giving me the too familiar line of asking me out for some wine and dine, tumble into the sack kind of thing that so many men do. He lived up to all my hopes.

"When Dale rang my doorbell, he was nervous, no doubt about it, even though we'd known each other so long. Never having seen a shy day my life, I fell right back into talking about the old days, about his family, and what we'd both been doing since we'd seen each other.

"It was like I'd found a long-lost friend that I'd never really had before — really weird but in a good way.

"We went to the movie, a film most tough-guy type men would put down as 'a woman's movie,' since it was a love story. Later, we went to a hamburger joint and had supper. It was great.

"Back at my door, he almost left before I could ask him to come in for a beer.

"But we sat there on the couch, picking up the conversation where we left off before the movie, and I felt more safe and secure than I had since I was a little girl. Here was a man that was nice, caring and holding my hand.

"I don't consider myself easy, but I swear I would have slept with him that night if he'd asked or tried. Not surprisingly, he didn't. In fact, he said something like, 'I'm still getting over my girlfriend, and I don't want to do anything on the rebound. When I feel a little more sure of myself and what I want to do, maybe we can see more of each other.'

"He was so down-home honest, I didn't know whether he was real or if he didn't care that much about seeing me again.

"A month later, he called back. When he asked if I'd like to go out again, I instantly said yes. That's when we really started dating, and before long, we were seeing each other every chance we could get.

"I have to say it wasn't the 'red roses' kind of romance. He sent me flowers for my birthday, but they were yellow roses, my favorite. From there on, it was like being in love with my best friend. It was wonderful.

"We were married a year later."

As the years have passed, Amanda says she sometimes misses the parties and night life she used to know, but if it came down to a trade in, she would stay where she is, anytime.

"He doesn't surprise me with sexy outfits and we don't go out partying, unless it's dinner with friends.

"But I never have to sit up waiting and wondering when or if he'll be home. I'll know he'll be home when he says he will.

"I love him so much, as much for the way he treats me, as for the way he's always ready to help anybody — whoever needs it.

"As far as our life goes now, I admit there are times I miss some of the things I used to enjoy, like going to the symphony or art shows, but I wouldn't trade what I have for anything."

HOW TO HANDLE THIS MAN

Unlike most men, this type of man is few and far between. The key to keeping him lies in what a woman really wants in a relationship.

If mink coats and facelifts are in her soul, this is not her dream lover. However, for women who want kindness, companionship and security, this is the lucky man. Those women must do two things to balance his home and hearth while maintaining respect for her own feelings. First, find ways to bring him out, at least occasionally, to do the things you enjoy. Second, appreciate what you have and look objectively at what you could lose.

This man will never accept dishonesty. He does not understand it. He can never condone adultery. It is not part of his constitution. He will not compromise his values for anyone, not even the woman he loves most dearly.

For these reasons, a woman who loves this kind of man must be true, first to herself and then to him. She must have the strength to resist what he would consider "hair-brained" desires to become a part of the social set or drive cars that cost as much as small houses.

No matter how much money or fame either person in this relationship may encounter in their own careers, family comes first, no questions asked. If it is a choice between helping others or building a pool, helping others will win.

A woman in love with this man must be

capable, if not of matching his high standards, of at least maintaining a vibrant respect for his ideals. If so, a woman who catches the heart of this man will reap mountains of love, becoming one of the happiest women you will ever meet. But, in order to do so, she must chalk up her childhood dreams of a dashing knight in shining armor for exactly what they were — fairy tales.

This man will be the first to acknowledge that he is no prince, simply a man who loves a woman and wants love in return.

"I know I'm one of the luckiest women alive," Amanda adds. "I know who he is and what he stands for. And he knows who I am and what I stand for. Most importantly, we respect each other.

"I've learned real gold doesn't necessarily glitter. It's more like a warm fire on a winter night."

MAN HANDLING TIPS

1. Remember how glad Dorothy was to return home from Oz.

2. Take your mother to the symphony.

3. Cheat on him and you're as good as gone.

CHAPTER VI

Mr. Born-To-The-Wild

Traits: Physical Strength
Rugged
Head-Strong

Likes: The Outdoors
Boats
Trucks

Dislikes: Snobbery
Telephones
Shaving

His Ideal Woman: Playful
Earthy
Thrifty

HIS PROFILE

Call him grizzly, call him a mountain man, but don't call him home until he is ready to come inside.

This man often acts as if he were reared by a pack of wolves. There is a part of the wild running through his veins, often making him comparable to an Alaskan Malamute or some other kind of creature that is gorgeous, yet not one hundred percent domesticated.

As a lover, in the true sense of the word, there is none better. His innate connection to nature carries over into the bedroom where he lovingly stalks his way to captivate his mate.

Mr. Born-to-The Wild is extremely territorial. Like a wolf, he is protective of his children.

Other people's children, even step-children, will more often be tolerated than adored. This is his natural way.

The same territorialism is equally important when a woman is considering him as long-time lover or husband material. He will protect *his* wife, *his* children and *his* home territory with his last ounce of muscle. At the same time, any woman who joins his pack will have to endure fishing worm containers in the refrigerator and accept that the only candlelight dinners will be canned beef stew around the campfire. His best trait is that he has the rare ability to love one woman, totally and forever.

ELLEN'S STORY

"When I met Charlie, I was 36 years old and had a four-year-old son. I had been divorced two years and was struggling from paycheck to paycheck to keep up," says Ellen, a secretary in Albuquerque.

"The last thing I needed was for a thunderstorm to crash over my house, ripping off half of the clay tiles. I met Charlie when I picked his construction company out of the yellow pages. That was on a Thursday, and he came over the following Saturday afternoon.

"I was so worried about money and trying to raise my son without a father that I had never given much thought to finding another man. My husband had walked out shortly after the birth of our son Sean, so I had neither the urge nor the time to start dating again.

"When Charlie pulled his truck into the driveway, I was outside mowing the lawn with an old push mower. I was hot, sweaty and wearing the oldest shorts and most ragged shirt I owned. I'm sure I looked and smelled like an old mop.

"Charlie didn't seem to notice. He hopped

out of his truck with a big smile on his face. Before he said a word, he grabbed the mower away from me and finished mowing a tricky little bank at the side of the house.

"Thirty minutes later, we were sitting at my kitchen table drinking iced tea. Within three days, I was in love with him. He fixed the roof, cleaned the gutters and fixed the commode in the downstairs bath.

"It was like God had sent him to me.

"In retrospect, I know I moved in on him like a vampire. In my defense, it had been so long since anybody had done things like that for me, I was like a sticktight. I did not want to let go."

In the first few weeks, Ellen says Charlie did not seem to mind her constant attention. But, as time passed, he seemed to be moving further away rather than closer.

"I started getting bitchy if he failed to call at least once a day, even when I knew he was out camping in the woods alone," she says. "I now recall him trying to tell me how much being outside, up in the mountains or on the lake fishing, meant to him. I refused to listen. I wanted him with me every minute of every day.

"We had been together about four months when everything blew up. The phone was ringing when I walked in the door from work, and it was Charlie. He said he was going out fishing for a while and would pick up a pizza and come over later.

"Before I could stop myself, I asked him when 'later' was.

"There was a long, dead silence. Then he said, 'I'm not sure. Let's just make it another time.' And then he hung up.

"I was stunned at first, then mad at him and finally mad at me. I ended up crying all night, and I didn't hear from him for days. My mind was filled with every thought imaginable. I envisioned him out partying with friends. Or, even worse, with another woman.

"Finally, I could stand it no more, so I called him. He sounded as if nothing had happened. I thought I was going crazy. It was Friday night and my son was at his dad's house for the weekend, so I asked him to come over. Within an hour, Charlie's truck came bouncing up the driveway.

"I was trembling as he walked in, but within minutes we were in bed, and I was trying to forget there had ever been a problem. He stayed all weekend, kissing me good-bye on his way to work Monday morning.

"When he was halfway out the door, I couldn't help but ask him when he'd be back. He gave me a look that clearly said, 'You are not my mother.' Then he walked out the door.

"I haven't heard from him since."

HOW TO HANDLE THIS MAN

No man likes a spider woman weaving clinging webs around him.

Clinging is a kiss of death to any relationship because clinging, nagging, bitching, etc., intrinsically denotes a woman's lack of self-image and self-respect.

There are countless ways to accomplish the same end to clinging — having your man around when you want him — without turning into a blubbering basket-case.

In Ellen's case, she was clearly insecure because of her ex-husband's abrupt exit. It is no wonder she wanted to latch on to Charlie and not let go even if lightning struck.

She simply went about it all wrong.

In the first place, this type of self-made, self-kept, and self-protected outdoors man needs a friendly guide through a relationship, not a gatekeeper.

The concept of time to a man who finds his

strength and direction in the open sky, means nothing beyond sunrise and sunset. When this man says he will be somewhere, he will be, but trying to clock him to an exact hour only makes him rebellious and resentful. What if the fish are biting? What if the buck he has been tracking is almost within his sights? What if the roof he's repairing takes longer to fix than he had estimated?

This free-spirited man needs a woman who is confident enough within herself not to worry about the clock. She must be a woman who trusts him until given a legitimate reason not to do so. And, if she wants to keep him, she must love him along with his restless spirit.

It is not easy to be such a confident, earthy woman. Some women cannot do it. Others refuse to do it because they do not deem changes in their own attitude worth keeping this kind of man.

In Ellen's situation, after failing to hear from Charlie for almost two months, she made the decision that she wanted to give it a try. She called, invited him over but had a surprise waiting — she was sitting on the front porch holding a fishing pole, with her canvass bag and ice cooler packed and ready to go camping.

"That weekend turned out to be a real turnaround in our relationship. Out on the lake, I told him without whining or anything, why I felt so insecure sometimes. Without me even asking, he told me that it made him feel trapped whenever I tried to pin him down all the time.

"We agreed on what we called 'our pact' to give it another try.

"When we have plans to get together, he's promised to tell me as close as he can when to expect him, and I promised not to get teary-eyed every time we kiss good-bye."

Today, a year into their "new" relationship, Ellen says she has never been happier.

"It took me this long to realize he could have been the kind of guy who was always late because he was hanging out in bars, flirting with other women," she says with a smile. "Just think of it, I was jealous of fish!

"He now comes and goes with friendly estimates of when to expect him, something I realized I should have done all along. While I don't plan on spending the rest of my life outdoors, I'm planning on enjoying the time we spend together, inside or out."

MAN HANDLING TIPS

1. If you must cling, grab a pillow.

2. Trust him.

3. Find something you like to do to put meaning into those hours spent waiting for him.

CHAPTER VII

Mr. Don't-Miss-Your-Chance

Traits: Brash
Arrogant
Confident

Likes: Work
Play
Head Games

Dislikes: Normalcy
Underdogs
Disarray

His Ideal Woman: Head Strong
Vibrant
Optimistic

HIS PROFILE

If there ever was a man who needs drop-kicking every once in a while, here he is. He can be the most arrogant, narcissistic and pretentious fellow you will ever meet. Everything about him, even the way he dresses — suspenders or vests are real popular with him — oozes with his grandiose visions of himself. While his inflated ego may be a turnoff for some, more than a few women will find him bizarrely attractive and intriguing.

Despite his arrogance, Mr.-Don't-Miss-Your-Chance does not lack a soft side. But, you will need a bull dozer to dig through all the tough outer layers to find it.

The good news is that he possesses the ability, both financially and intellectually, to take you on the ride of your life, whether you are his girlfriend or his wife. Any woman who tries it needs to do an inventory of her own abilities to ensure she is up to the challenge.

If you are a woman who is bothered by confrontations, you will be much better off letting this man pass you by. If, however, you consider yourself a contender when the need arises, snap on your seat belt and prepare for the ride of your life.

SUE'S STORY

"I watched Mark from the back of the courtroom during the three-day trial," says Sue, 32, a Boston lobbyist for a health care reform group.

"Did he ever strut! He reminded me of a peacock, wrapping his thumbs around his suspenders and sticking out his chest as he grilled witness after witness. But I will be the first to admit that he is one helluva lawyer. Sharp. Quick. With all the right moves in the courtroom. You could tell he played the jury to the hilt.

"It was a malpractice suit. I had no doubt that his client was guilty, but I could tell he was probably going to win. He was that good."

When the judge adjourned the case for the weekend, Sue went back to her office, picked up the phone and called Mark. She wanted to arrange a meeting between her group and him to discuss an upcoming conference on the ramifications of malpractice suits on physicians' insurance rates.

"His secretary put me through. I politely told him who I was and what I wanted," she says.

"Suddenly, he launched into this verbal attack of me, my organization and the conference. I was so taken aback, I'm surprised I kept my cool, but I did. Ignoring his outburst, I thanked him for his time and hung up.

"What an ass!" I thought to myself as I began looking for another attorney, without such an attitude, who would attend the conference. That would have been the last of the conversation if had fate not intervened.

"A week or two later I was returning home from a business trip from Miami. I boarded the plane, sat in an aisle seat in first class and began to sip a glass of wine prior to takeoff when Mark got on the plane. He glanced my way, but had no way of knowing who I was since we had never met face to face.

"He removed his jacket — there were those damn suspenders — and sat down across the aisle a row in front of me. The plane eventually took off, and even though I had planned to work through the three hour flight, I kept staring at the back of his head, seething about the phone call.

"I had managed to get myself completely worked up by the time we landed in Boston. I would have loved to have strangled him, but I told myself he wasn't worth the time. I'm not sure what came over me as we were walking up the jet-way into the terminal.

"Out of nowhere, I tapped him sharply on the shoulder and in a rush of words told him who I was, that I thought his tirade on the telephone was inexcusable and that I wanted him to know the world was not nearly as taken by him as he was of himself. Then I stomped away.

"I was greatly surprised when I heard him calling my name, trying to catch me. When he did, he was very apologetic, and asked me to have a drink and talk things over. I had already consumed too much wine, apparently, because I told him there was no way in hell I wanted to spend another minute of my time with him. Then I told him to get a life and I walked on."

Three dozen red roses arrived at Sue's office the next morning. The card read "D.S.F."

Mark called before noon.

"Thanks," I said, "but what's this D.S.F. thing?"

"Desperately Seeking Forgiveness," he said shyly. "How about dinner?"

So began what appeared to be a fairy tale.

"He picked me up in his Rolls, and we went straight to the airport, caught a private jet and flew to New York for dinner," Sue says. "I had been courted before, but nothing that could compare to this.

"For the next few weeks, the courtship continued. One incredible romantic runaway after another. You should have heard the verbal sparring between us. It was great fun. We disagreed about almost everything, as far as politics or public policies go, but the banter between us was great. It took some effort, but I loved it when I got him in a philosophical bind that he had to fight himself out of.

"Talk, however, was about all we did. He left after every nightcap, without more than a few hot kisses at the door.

"It is difficult to explain, but I made it a point not to sleep with him. He was certainly attractive, but I wasn't comfortable with the idea. Something told me that if I slept with him, things would never be the same.

"I don't know if I was scared that I might fall in love with him or if I was unsure whether or not I could hold onto him if I did.

"The time finally arrived when I had to make the decision, one way or another. He wanted us to go to Europe and take the Orient Express, the luxurious train ride to the Far East. I knew if we were on a train together for 10 days, there would be more than kisses at the door."

HOW TO HANDLE THIS MAN

Sue's instincts were right on target. Under the circumstances of their first meeting, she knew that maintaining a long-term relationship with Mark would take a lot of work.

First, keeping this man's attention is a day-by-day task because in many ways he is too smart, too secure and too self-important for his own good. Being nice is not what he is about. He is about making sure his life is full of sparks.

He does not discuss. He makes opening and closing arguments.

He refuses to court a woman with love notes. He sweeps her off the runway with alluring real-life fantasies.

And he will not promise anything beyond the thrill of it all.

For Sue, though she had proven she could hang in there with him and be a contender, she decided that she preferred to look for a different kind of man — one who would no doubt offer less fireworks but more peaceful moments.

"It was the right decision for me," she says. "After I explained why I was unable to go to Europe or start in a more serious relationship with him, Mark actually saw my point. I believe he respected me for making the decision before things went too far.

"It has been six years since then. I have married, as has he. About once a year, I get a call from him. He doesn't have to say it, but I can tell he's still looking for adventure, which tells me his wife is struggling to keep up with him.

"I'm glad it's her and not me."

When all is said and done, women who want to find happiness with this man must at the same time accept the assignment of a lifetime of keeping up with him, mentally and romantically.

Susan Thomas

MAN HANDLING TIPS

1. Never assume the quest is completed.

2. Keep him on his toes.

3. Be his contender.

CHAPTER VIII

Mr. Hello-In-There

Traits: Skeptical
Dogmatic
Tough-Skinned

Likes: Freedom
Quiet Times
Rainy Days

Dislikes: Differing Opinions
Control
Pompousness

His Ideal Woman: Independent
Empathetic
Practical

HIS PROFILE

Is he lonely or a loner?

You cannot quite put your finger on it when you first meet this man, but you know there is something different about him — not in the way he looks, talks or dresses, but different in the sense that something faraway is lurking inside. This intangible feeling emits a subtle sadness that creeps out of his words or the look in his eyes. He brings out the gentle, nurturing side of any woman.

Often, he puts up a rugged exterior that can turn off even the most tenderhearted woman. This outer shell is only his defense against exposing his true feelings, the deep secret he carries beneath the surface.

This man is difficult to handle in the early

going because getting to know him is like trying to connect with a computer without a modem. Conversation is easy and light, but getting past his defenses appears impossible. If, however, that barrier is penetrated by a woman who cares enough to invest the time, what awaits her — delving into a world he has refused to let anyone share for a long time — can be magical.

Once that journey begins, handling this man is as natural as the changing seasons.

GLORIA'S STORY

"I met Max through friends at a Fourth of July party at the lake," says Gloria, 32, a telephone operator in a small town in Illinois. "Everyone was in couples except us, so we gravitated towards each other.

"Our small talk was predictable. I told him about my job, and he told me he was a veteran and that he worked in administration at a local factory.

"We weren't particularly shy, but our conversation kept coming back to things like the weather. It was like talking to a stranger in line at a grocery store. But, there was something about Max that made me want to get closer. I just didn't know how."

As the evening progressed, Max asked Gloria if she would like to take a ride in his boat so that they could watch the fireworks show from the water.

"It sounded neat, so we put a few beers in the cooler on the boat and took off. We rode around for about thirty minutes and it was too loud to talk, so I relaxed and enjoyed the fresh air. When we saw the first fireworks, Max pulled the boat a little towards the shore and tossed out the anchor.

"The fireworks were beautiful. We

watched with little conversation. When one very bright stream of light fell on his face, I could have sworn I saw tears in his eyes. It hit me straight in the heart. Naturally, I was embarrassed to say anything, yet I wondered why he seemed so sad."

Gloria said she and Max saw each other occasionally during the next few weeks. Despite those meetings, Gloria admits she knew little more about him than she had known on that first night.

"As I spent more time with him, I began to really like him," she says. "One night, while we were on his boat, I asked him why he didn't have a steady girlfriend. I tried to say it as lightheartedly as possible, but he became immediately serious.

"He said he had been married once and that he was so set in his ways, he had no plans to ever remarry. He was only 41. That's fairly young to write off the rest of your love life.

"When he saw my expression, he was very polite and said if he ever thought about getting serious again, it would be with someone like me. I was flattered, but more curious than ever. Before that night ended, he told me politely that he would like to have a relationship with me but that he wanted me to know from the start that commitment to one woman was not in his plans.

"I respected him for that. At least he was honest. But it only made me want him more."

Though some would call it devious, Gloria's next move was something she felt she had to do. It was necessary for her and for whatever future she might have with Max.

"I called one of his friends," she says. "I wanted to find out if Max was completely against commitments to women because of a bad relationship in the past or if there was some other reason. If he had been burned, I could live with that and write him off. But if it was something else, I needed to know."

Gloria's hunch paid off. Though the friend would say little, she learned that Max was a Viet Nam veteran who, while having accepted the war as part of his past, had never accepted the cold shoulder the country had shown him and his friends who never made it home.

"It don't think Max trusts anybody or anything," the friend had said.

"There was a part of me that said 'give it up,'" Gloria recalls. "When I thought about it, it wasn't like I was fighting some woman's ghost from the past. I was fighting a hurt that didn't have anything to do with women. It was bigger than that. I hoped that enough years had passed that Max might be able to come to grips with a part of history that most Americans are ashamed of."

Gloria persisted, and ever so slowly, Max began to talk about the war every now and then.

"It was months — maybe even a year — before he finally told me all about what he had gone through, how he had watched his friends die only to come back home to jeers, not cheers, of people putting down the war," Gloria says.

"I was honest with him. I told him I couldn't imagine how he felt or what the war had done to him. After I stopped talking, he hugged me so hard and for so long, I could hardly breathe. It was wonderful."

HOW TO HANDLE THIS MAN

Since the initial handling of this man is treacherous and can be so laborious, many woman refuse to even attempt to undertake such a task. That is often for the best since many of these men will never recover from their past and return to the world.

Their reasons run the gamut — be it the

loss of a loved one, guilt over something over which they had no control, bitterness over a lost trust. Or, as in Max's case, a real-life war and its empty aftermath.

Lonely or a loner? This man is both. For that reason, if a woman takes the time to find out the cause of his pain, chances are she will reap this man's love and attention at that moment, as well as the years of love he has locked away for so long.

"Max and I have recently started living together," Gloria says. "The past three years haven't been easy. The first one was especially tough.

"With my encouragement, Max returned to Viet Nam with several of his Army buddies last fall. He told me that it was too intense to try to explain with words. Since he's been back, little things have changed. He is much more open about his feelings. He's able to talk about the feelings he's had over the years and he shows much more affection than before.

"I know he will never get over what he went through. However, I now know he is trying to say good-bye to the past as well as trying to do a little more living in the present.

"I just thank my lucky stars I stayed around him long enough to share today with him."

MAN HANDLING TIPS

1. Take it slow and easy.

2. Read behind his eyes.

3. Tell him you care.

CHAPTER IX
Mr. Can-We-Say-Ma-Ma?

Traits: Young
Trusting
Adventurous

Likes: Sports
Motorcycles
Sex

Dislikes: Parents
Rules
Pimples

His Ideal Woman: Worldly
Supple
Buxom

HIS PROFILE

He must have been a beautiful baby.

This child-man can be every older woman's fantasy: Soft skin. Tight muscles. Trusting. Sweet. Never more than a second away from sex, yet years away from wrinkles, beer bellies and attitudes.

What seems to be too good to be true usually is. This baby, who has, at least in his young heart, fallen desperately in love with you, is no exception.

Unless you have enough money to continually fill in every dimple of cellulite, smooth every wrinkle, tuck every crease and still have enough money to live like you are twenty-two, be gentle with this boy.

He is young and naive. He breaks easily.

Unfortunately, that only enhances his attraction.

ELIZABETH'S STORY

"This is the most bizarre story," says Elizabeth, a 33-year-old mother of two adolescent sons.

"Last year, my sister, who also has children, offered to serve as a host to an exchange student from France. Her husband was transferred out of state in April, so she asked me if I would mind having the young man live with my children and me during his six weeks in the states. I was divorced and struggling to do the best I could with my own kids, so I really didn't want to. But, there was really no other alternative, so I grudgingly agreed.

"I didn't want him to be disappointed, and I thought he would enjoy begin with my two boys."

It did not happen that way.

"His name was Laurent," Elizabeth remembers. "He was sixteen, several years older than my boys, and spoke only enough English to say hello. At the airport, I immediately felt I had made a mistake.

"In the first few days, he tried to integrate with my boys and their friends, but beyond shooting basketball in the backyard, they had nothing in common. I soon found myself sitting with Laurent, French-English and English-French dictionaries in hand, trying desperately to communicate.

"I was surprised when I started enjoying his company. Each time we could find enough words to construct a sentence and communicate with each other was a big victory."

One night, after she thought her sons and Laurent were fast asleep, Elizabeth walked outside to the swing she and her ex-husband had assembled, together, while talking of the days in the decades to come when they would sit there watching their grandchildren play.

"I started crying," Elizabeth says. "No big sobs, merely tears for something that was never going to be. I wasn't still in love with my ex. I suppose I was just lonely.

"In mid-thought, I looked up and saw Laurent. I made a feeble attempt to smile, but he could see I was crying. He sat down beside me in the swing. Since we were in the dark without our dictionaries, there was literally no conversation. We just sat there, swinging for a while, then he reached over and held my hand.

"I didn't stop him. Actually, I believe I held his hand tighter than he did mine."

The next morning, Elizabeth found an envelope on the kitchen counter. In broken English, it read, "My love is you."

"I had never imagined myself in a situation where a boy half my age would be attracted to me," she says, obviously embarrassed. "It was surreal, most of all because I did have a certain attraction to him that had nothing to do with our ages. He was just so sweet, so caring, so loving.

"I found myself feeling very sad that he was so young and I wasn't."

HOW TO HANDLE THIS MAN

To this day, Elizabeth says she still has feelings of regret that are difficult to explain. She says she regrets that she did not let the relationship with Laurent go any further than it did. At the same time, she often regrets that any connection happened at all.

In any relationship with this kind of boy, chances are the woman will bear the morning after thoughts, alone, as this young man starts out in search of that "girl" of his dreams.

There are exceptions. Some few wealthy women can surgically remove their age for an extended time. But the truth is that most women age with the years, mentally and physically. It is not only that their bodies are not exactly what they used to be, but more importantly, it is that they have developed a mature respect for this child-man who they know needs to grow in his own time, at his own pace, and with a woman his own age.

The fact is, it is easy for an older woman to command a child-man's attention for a time. Remember, however, that time is on *his* side. If an older woman places her stakes on keeping a younger man for long, she will lose. When she loses, her wrinkles will seem deeper and her bulges will seem bigger because she is comparing them to a time when time was on her side.

The best bet is to be gentle and kind to this child-man, and wish him well as you send him off in search of his own love in his own generation.

MAN HANDLING TIPS

1. Restrain yourself!

2. Relish the thought of a boy's fascination with you.

3. Kiss him good-bye — on the cheek.

CHAPTER X

Mr. Mentor-Me-Too

Traits: Older
              Secure
              Controlling

Likes: Giving Advice
              Talking
              Adoration

Dislikes: Rebellion
              Loss of Control
              Aging

His Ideal   Young
Woman: Eager
              Emotionally Needy

HIS PROFILE

He is the father you either always or never had, except that he is much better. He is wiser, more understanding, more caring, more handsome in his own special way, more loving, more *everything*. You wonder how you made it this far without him. You are absolutely terrified of attempting to make it any further if you fail to follow his lead.

He is your mentor. Your worldly god. He is going to protect you, help you, support you, encourage you to do your best — up until the time you have matured enough to take care of yourself.

That is when things can get complicated with this mentoring man.

More often than not, this man is exactly what he appears to be. He is older, wiser and more than willing to help. What is difficult to predict is the way in which he will react when you reach the point when you no longer need his nurturing nest.

LINDA'S STORY

"Thomas has done more for me than I could ever have asked or expected anyone to do," says Linda, 35, a family physician in Little Rock.

"Without his encouragement, I might have settled for being a physical therapist instead of a physician, which was what I really wanted to be. He was wonderful as far as encouragement goes.

"In the beginning, even though he tried to come off as gruff, he was prodding me to keep me on the path that I really wanted to follow. He played the devil's advocate role well, and that made me want to work even harder for what I really wanted to do with my life.

"For that, I will love him forever.

"The trouble, if you can call it that, started when I had almost completed medical school. For five years, I had listened to Thomas intently, made sure I was available for any dinner parties he and his wife threw, and in general, jumped whenever he called.

"Our sexual relationship evolved; I certainly didn't plan it. It started as a hug and then a kiss, and then the rest followed. I was realistic and never considered thoughts of our future together, but I suppose a part of me wanted to show him how much I appreciated his help, and lovemaking was my way of doing that.

"It wasn't a lurid affair. We were only together sexually about half a dozen times, usually when we were on the road traveling together to conferences. Every now and then I'd feel a guilt streak because of his wife, and I continue to have a little sinking feeling about that today. All in all, it was something that happened, and I was so caught up in school and trying to make it, I rarely dated anyone.

"Suddenly, I found a boyfriend. He was not somebody I was ready to marry. He was simply a guy to go out with and have fun.

"You should have heard Thomas when he found out about this guy, who was a fellow student of mine. That night, Thomas was in another state giving a lecture after which he called me. He was like a tornado tearing up the telephone.

"Not only did he tell me that I was making the worse decision of my life, he also started saying that maybe he had been wrong about me, after all. That perhaps I would have made a better therapist than a doctor.

"I was livid.

"I slammed down the phone, and without a moment's thought, I drove to the airport, caught a plane to the city where he was, got a taxi to his hotel and knocked on his door about two a.m.

"He sleepily opened the door, enough for me to barge in screaming. I dared him to give me hell, in person, over a boyfriend he did not even know. I told him he was a real jerk for trying to put me down when I had always followed his advice.

"He was just standing there, in his boxer shorts, stunned.

"It wasn't funny to me then, but it is now.

"He said, 'Are you finished?' I said, 'I guess.' And then he came over, hugged me, and kissed me on the mouth, hard.

"I couldn't help saying, 'Listen mister, if you want to kiss me, slow down and enjoy it.'

"He said, 'So you're all grown up now and you're going to tell me how to kiss, too?' I answered, 'Guess so.'

"Then we made love, for the last time."

HOW TO HANDLE THIS MAN

The subject of sex is difficult to avoid in most mentoring relationships, whether any physical consummation ever occurs. It stems from the electricity automatically generated by success, that held by the mentor and that coveted by the protege. It is an exciting time when someone is learning and someone is teaching, and that wellspring heightens every nerve, including the libido.

Morals aside, the potential complications for a female protege are innumerable. The complications can range from the sexual component overshadowing the original intent of the relationship to the double control handed over to the mentor when a woman puts both her future and her body in his hands.

For that reason, the woman who decides to dabble in romance with her mentor must always keep her focus toward her future goals. She must make it clear, and stand behind her conviction that any physical relationship is no more than that, and never will be.

Falling in love with a mentor is potentially professional suicide. Any indication that a protege may become a threat to his status or his home life, which almost always includes a wife, usually ends in disaster. The protege is dropped and any investment on her part up until that time is wasted.

In a perfect world, the best way for a woman to handle a mentor is at arm's length. As time passes, so does the heat of the moment, and a healthy respect for one another can go a long way in the years ahead. Since there are few situations in which sexual temptation is greater, if a physical relationship occurs, the woman must be capable of keeping it in perspective. She must let her mentor know that she fully realizes the day will come when she grows her own wings and flies away. At that point, she expects their relationship to mature into one of friendship and mutual respect — though she will always carry with her gratitude for his nurturing.

MAN HANDLING TIPS

1. Appreciate him as a mentor, not a god.

2. Make sure he plays fair.

3. Lay the foundation for friendship, not him.

CHAPTER XI

Mr. I'm-Too-Sexy-For-My-Socks

Traits:
    Gorgeous
    Futuristic
    Gracious

Likes:
    Adoration
    Sincerity
    Loyalty

Dislikes:
    Possessiveness
    Selfishness
    Visionless

His Ideal Woman:
    Refined
    Logical
    Diplomatic

HIS PROFILE

He is to die for.

He causes an overwhelming rush the minute he walks into the room.

He is *man*.

He is the flesh and blood version of the romance novel cover. His body would be envied by any Greek god. His thick, rich hair has never known a split end. His eyes are so deep and so sensuous and they seem to be searching — for you.

Meet the man of your dreams.

But, before you leave your boyfriend or file for divorce, your best bet is to take a reality check.

What's beneath that incredible male veneer?

GINA'S STORY

"Hi, sexy."

"Those were the first two words he ever said to me," says Gina, 21, a college student in Tampa. "I thought I was going to melt.

"He was so good looking. Meeting him was like walking down the beach one day and finding the prince I had dreamed would sweep me off my feet and take me off into the sunset to live happily ever after.

"His name was Zach, and I was in heaven."

Days passed. Zach spent every one of them with her. Gina says she wore a permanent smile.

"I was so happy," she says. "Every moment with him was wonderful, and the anticipation of our next moment together was as good.

"It was as if every inch of me was alive, and falling in love.

"I knew that I was young, much too young to begin thinking of marriage. Even though Zach was twenty-six, he, too, was too young to start thinking about marriage. We knew that we were young, we were happy, and we were having a whole lot of fun. If anything, that was what I wanted, and I didn't want anything to change.

"Zach was a studio musician in Tampa, so we were able to go to all the concerts free and go a lot of places where I wouldn't have been able to go otherwise.

"I loved the parties his musician friends threw. They were crazy, totally crazy, and completely unpredictable. It was a blast!"

Gina and Zach had dated exactly six months nonstop, the night she sneaked up behind him to kiss him on the back of the neck during a beach party.

"He was standing there, and a record label saleswoman was walking up to him," Gina recalls. "I thought I would kiss him and join in their conversation, but I was a couple of steps behind him when she walked up. Then I heard him say 'Hi Sexy' to her.

"It was like someone had thrown a glass of cold water in my face. Those were the very first words he had said to me, and I had thought I was something special."

Gina made a decision at that moment that very few women, particularly at her young age, would have had the sense to make. Without hesitation, she proceeded with the unexpected kiss on the back of Zach's neck. Beyond that, she never let him know that she had heard his greetings to the saleswoman.

Instead, she smiled and let the moment pass.

Then a few days later, she decided to drop a bomb of her own.

"I told Zach that I had been thinking it over and that we had gotten too close too soon and I wanted to let things cool down a little," she says. "Actually, after that night on the beach, it was true. I knew that if he thought I would be willing to stand on the sidelines while he romanced, or at least subtly enticed other women, he would take advantage of me until he moved on to someone else.

"I wasn't willing to do that, not even for Zach."

HOW TO HANDLE THIS MAN

There are a few men who are just too good looking for their own good.

Unfortunately, their striking physical appearance presents a double dilemma. It gives them a carte blanche card to be a heel — but at the same time can overshadow anything else they may have going for them, like being a decent person.

Finding what lies beneath this man's beauty is the trick. Figuring out the ways to accomplish that task can be even trickier.

In Gina's case, she had the grit to grasp early that she did not intend to be a face in the crowd, cheering Zach on. She would either be with him, as the woman he wanted most, or she would not be there at all. That is the best any woman can do with a man whose good looks and charm could captivate most any woman any time.

The key is that this man, despite his outward appearance, needs a woman who is able to see beneath the flesh. It takes a woman who can calculate the difference between being a good-looking person and being a good person.

Today, a year after Gina met Zach, they are closer than ever before.

"I know him now, beyond a gorgeous reflection in the mirror," she says. "He knows me, too. He knows how much I care about the real him, not just the way he looks. But, he knows that I'll be gone if he gets so caught up in the way he looks that he forgets the person he is inside.

"When we go to the beach now, I still see women looking at him and drooling. When I look at him, he seems to be a lot more concerned with the guys who are looking at me."

MAN HANDLING TIPS

1. Look beneath the surface.

2. Remember that pretty is as pretty does.

3. Let him chase you.

CHAPTER XII

Mr. Forget-Me-Not

Traits: Absent Minded
Disorganized
Indecisive

Likes: TV Dinners
Naps
Fishing

Dislikes: Lists
Clocking In
Talking on the Phone

His Ideal Woman: Liberal
Unselfish
Generous

HIS PROFILE

From your first meeting, you are convinced this man needs you.

He stumbles, rather than walks, through life, aimlessly wandering around in circles with no clear destination. He talks of things he has thought of doing but never got around to. His home is full of little projects begun but never completed. He has every intention of fixing the dripping faucet in the bathroom, but says he has grown fond of the steady drip, drop, drip when he goes to bed.

You can size him up easily. All he needs is a good woman to lead him through life.

What many women fail to realize is that a man who has trouble keeping up with himself will also have trouble coming through with those simple little things in life that most all people want and need — like being appreciated.

BETH'S STORY

"I'll admit it," says Beth, 33, a court reporter in San Francisco, "I met John and decided I had been placed upon this earth to save him from himself.

"He was so sweet, in a bumbling kind of way, never quite sure where he left his glasses or what time we were supposed to meet. I learned a long time ago that the key to my heart is for a man to need me, and I had never met anybody who seemed to need more tender loving care than John.

"Once we started dating, he began to depend on me for everything, and I loved it. I decided what we'd have for dinner. I decided what movie we would go see. I picked out his clothes to wear the next morning. I made sure the doors were locked and his cigarette was out before we went to bed at night.

"Eventually we moved in together. Perhaps I was playing mother to the child I'd never had. As time passed, I took charge of his life and enjoyed it. Now, I think it was more of a situation where his dependence on me helped me validate my own life. I felt I was a better person because I was taking care of both of us.

"Slowly but surely, I helped him finish or throw out all the little things around his house that never really got off the ground, like finishing painting the kitchen, putting together a bookcase and labeling the stacks of VCR tapes of movies he'd taped over the years but neglected to mark.

"I thought I was happy, but there were no big explosions in the lovemaking department. I didn't hear bells when he kissed me, but I thought I loved him and we had started talking about getting married.

"We had been together exactly one year when it hit me. I had gone to great lengths to remind him for weeks that our one year together was coming up, and we made plans to go out to dinner to a nice place.

"For weeks, I looked for the perfect present, every time I went shopping. I searched for something special, something that would have both a sentimental and a personal touch. After finding nothing in the stores, I thought of having the first picture of us together turned into a small line-drawing etching for his desk at work. I had it framed and loved it. It was so original, so classy, and I was proud of my creativity.

"I hadn't given a whole lot of thought to what he might get me. A diamond was in the back of my mind, but I'd already promised myself to act pleased with whatever he gave me. I hoped it was something personal, maybe a bracelet or necklace.

"Our anniversary day arrived. It was great because it was a Friday, and I left him a note when I left for work thanking him for one of the best years of my life. I wrote that I could hardly wait for dinner that night.

"We went to dinner at the Wharf, and it was great. When we finished, we were sitting there sipping coffee, looking out on the lights of the bay, when I handed him the gift-wrapped etching. He was like a little boy — so excited when I handed it to him. He tore open the paper and sat there staring at it, going on and on about how wonderful it was and how thoughtful I was.

"When he didn't give me my present before asking for the check, I got my hopes up that maybe it was going to be a diamond and he wanted to pick a more romantic setting in which to ask me to marry him.

"I waited. He didn't make a move outside along the peer, so I waited. When he asked if I was ready to go back home, I said sure, thinking the surprise waited there. When we got in the house, he kissed me all the way to the bedroom, and I waited. Then we made love, and he fell asleep.

"I was numb. I stared at the ceiling till I fell asleep. It wasn't until after breakfast the next morning that the truth sunk in. The creep didn't even buy me an anniversary gift of any kind."

Beth, unlike some more forceful women, never said a word. She hid her feelings from him, but says they were boiling inside of her. She was hurt and resentful. After everything she had done for him, their anniversary didn't mean enough to him to take the time to even buy her a card.

Her birthday was two months away. He took her to dinner and that was it.

"I was crushed," she says. "I had done everything for him, and what did I get from him? Nothing.

"When I told him I wanted to break up, he said he didn't understand. I left that week and it was over."

HOW TO HANDLE THIS MAN

Most men will get away with whatever they can.

The key lies solely in what the woman is willing to let him get away with.

A man who takes and takes without so much as a thank you is his own worst enemy. He will not become a woman's problem unless she lets him become a problem.

Yet, not all men are trained to show much outward affection, from words to cards, gifts or whatever. Therefore, it is up to a woman to gently yet firmly let him know that while she can live without big price-tag items, an occasional tangible token of love or appreciation would mean very much to her.

If a woman does that sincerely and honestly, there is no excuse for a man of any financial status not to respond.

Most of the very best gestures of love cost little.

A small bunch of wildflowers, picked on the spur of the moment without occasion, can touch the toughest woman's heart.

MAN HANDLING TIPS

1. Get involved at your own risk.

2. Set your limits and stick to them.

3. Buy his gifts for you with his credit card.

CHAPTER XIII

Mr. President

Traits: Determined
Self-Centered
Driven

Likes: Order
Winning
Admiration

Dislikes: Surprises
Chatter
Laziness

His Ideal Woman: Physical Beauty
Supportive
Seen But Not Heard

HIS PROFILE

This overachiever will never have quite enough — be it money or power, or encounters with woman. Often from a financially poor childhood, he is driven by a burning desire to become "somebody." No matter what he has achieved, he will never realize that his accomplishments are outstanding. If he could step out of his three piece suit once in a while, he would realize that he already has much more than most. However, he is incapable of such critical self-examination.

In that regard, he is as good as blind. That is why his preoccupation with getting further and further ahead continually overshadows his ability to enjoy the richness of the moment. He only finds that richness in immediate conquests — in the boardroom or the bedroom of another woman.

It is not that he does not love a "one and only." This man simply cannot resist the temptation to try to conquer everything he sees, including attractive women.

SHERRI'S STORY

"This is awful to say, but at first I felt like a real sleazebag," says Sherri, 27, an advertising account representative at a Chicago pharmaceuticals company.

"It's the same old story. A business trip. A drink at the bar that turned into five or six. Then I wake up with my boss, a very married boss.

"I had sworn that would never happen to me. I had seen girlfriends go through it and get hurt, and I just never imagined I would find myself in that spot.

"I didn't need to sleep with him to get ahead. I was doing just fine on my own. He wasn't even very good-looking!

"At first I tried to blame it on the vodka, but as those first days went by, I realized it was not him, but his power that attracted me to him. He was on his way to becoming CEO in a couple of years, no doubt about it, and everybody I work with respects him so much.

"Maybe I even saw him as a father figure.

"For the next few weeks we acted like nothing had happened, but my paranoia was incredible. I felt like I had a scarlet letter on my forehead and everybody was looking at me when I walked down the hall. In meetings, I would try to read everybody's face to see if anyone had a clue. Every time somebody said they needed to talk to me, I panicked, thinking it was about what had happened. But, nobody knew.

"Nothing happened for a while, so I just tried to forget that anything had ever happened.

I admit it was tough not thinking about him. If he hadn't have been married, I would have rated our night together pretty high up there in terms of the men I've known.

"But it seemed useless. I had seen his wife a couple of times at holiday parties. I had never really talked to her, but from the way she acted, she seemed like one of those society climbers.

"I knew I was smarter than to get involved with a married man."

About three months later, Sherri said she found herself in yet another out-of-town hotel room, with her boss knocking at the door.

"I asked him in awkwardly, letting him know I had no plans for another romp in bed. But that's when he dropped the bomb. He said he and his wife had drifted apart and that they were getting a divorce. Then he said he really cared about me.

"I really don't remember much about the rest of that night. All I know is that I knew I really cared about this guy, and even loved him.

"The next months were what I would call a happy hell. Everybody at the office found out we were seeing each other as soon as his divorce was filed. They had no children, so the whole thing was over pretty quickly, and I had a three-carat diamond on my hand and a huge wedding planned.

"Everything was wonderful until the night when we ran into his ex-wife at dinner.

"I saw her coming toward our table, and I could tell from her unsteady step that she had been drinking. She walked over and stopped right beside him. He looked up, bewildered, then she looked straight at me and said pleasantly, 'Remember one thing, Sweetie. If he strayed from my bed, he'll stray from yours.'

"I felt like someone had kicked me in the stomach. Part of my brain was screaming, 'You had better listen to what she said. She's probably right. What's going to stop him from playing around down the road after you've settled into the wife role?'

"I made him take me straight home. I wouldn't talk to him. I told him I needed some time to myself. He was as humble as he had ever been, apologizing for her and everything.

"I told him it wasn't his fault and to give me some space."

HOW TO HANDLE THIS MAN

Many more women have slept with their bosses than will ever admit it. Many others have slept with married men, boss or not. But few women get as far in this kind of a relationship as Sherri. The fact is, any woman who engages in a sexual relationship with this man might as well shoot herself in the foot. Any woman who believes she will eventually lure him to the altar might as well shoot the other foot while she's at it.

The truth is that no woman, over the long haul, will ever mean as much to this man as his job or his material possessions. That doesn't mean he is incapable of love. He can love, but to this man, love often translates into his desire — and need — to have a trophy woman to hang on his arm. That is as close as any woman is ever going to get.

Handling this man is tough, but for those determined to try it, realize first and foremost that you have to be as tough as he is.

The first hurdle is deciding if you can handle a life in which his Jaguar and job title place first and second before you. That is not to say that he cannot love you. He will, but it is a rather shallow love in comparison to others. By the same token, he will love any children and be proud of their accomplishments. However, he will prefer a live-in nanny rather than helping out with the dirty diapers.

It is also doubtful he will want you to continue a career. He has plenty of money to take care of both of you, and he would prefer you doing volunteer work. That not only makes him king of the financial roost, but your good deeds will reflect positively on him in the community.

This man wants a woman who will place him first, above all else. There are, of course, advantages to this man. He is smart and the money is in the bank. But if you want him — and want to keep him — you will have to be strong.

Most of all, you must discipline yourself. You must set out in your own mind the things you will and will not accept in his behavior. You must tell him your thoughts in order to see if he is prepared to make that commitment to you. If he is, the most important thing you must do is remain firm on your agreement. Never let him think that you will back down. *Ever.*

The key here is that he must know every hour of the day that you love him, but if he is ever tempted to take an illicit romp, his commitment is to tell you *before* an affair begins. In that case, explain that you will play fair in the divorce.

Otherwise, if he lies, you will take every damn thing he owns, including the Jag, his money and his three-piece suits. If this man truly knows that you are the type of woman to back up your words, odds are you will be happily married every after.

Sherri has been for almost sixteen years.

MAN HANDLING TIPS

1. Acknowledge you are playing with fire.

2. If he plays footsies under the table, make sure it is with your feet.

3. Never back down.

CHAPTER XIV
Mr. Roll-With-The-Dice

Traits: Deceptive
Coy
Exciting

Likes: Parties
Privacy
Surprises

Dislikes: Boredom
Routine
Taxes

His Ideal Woman: Vibrant
Outspoken
Gutsy

HIS PROFILE

This man is a gambler, and that risk taking streak will drive any woman nuts if she lets it. Life, to this man, is one big crap shoot, and he would not have it any other way.

His background is most often middle-class, a place where he learned early that it is entirely up to an individual to succeed or fail. He dislikes restraints and rules of any kind. He loves beating a speeding ticket, finding lucky pennies and passing himself off as being just a little bit better — on every level — than he really is. His outward disregard for regular people who play it safe stems from his own self-doubt, which he hides at all costs.

A woman capable of handling such a risk

taker must, ironically, be a risk taker herself. She must be able to see through his outer shell and still love what she sees. She must be able to put up with his lack of openness, knowing that if he professes his love, she is as close as anyone is ever going to get.

DENISE'S STORY

"I think Kirk thought he could get away with a lot just because I was younger than he was," says Denise, 33, a department store clerk in Little Rock.

"I met him through my boyfriend, who I was living with at the time. At first, Kirk flabbergasted me. He would go to Nassau or Las Vegas on a whim, or disappear for a week or two and then reappear. I had never been anywhere but Florida, so his traveling impressed me.

"Kirk managed a great Mexican restaurant in town — cozy but classy and great food. I was really surprised the first time he asked me over for dinner. He had stopped by while my boyfriend was a work and I thought he was asking me to come over and eat because I was alone.

"I didn't think about it at the time, but he started stopping by more and more in the afternoon, after my boyfriend had left for his second-shift job at a manufacturing company.

"Those first dinners with Kirk were so much fun. He had the strolling band play some outlandish Spanish love songs I didn't understand, while he mimicked the words in English. He was crazy and fun. Before I knew it, I had broken up with my boyfriend and was dating Kirk.

"It was wild. My mother hated him, probably because he was older. But the more she put him down, the more I stood up for him. You know how that goes.

"The first six or seven months were heaven. It was all I could do to keep my job because we were either staying up all night in bed or hopping on a plane heading for wherever gambling was legal.

"As naive as it sounds, I was unaware that gambling could be a sickness. Those first months, I would sit beside him at the blackjack table watching him win thousands of dollars only to see him lose it more quickly than he had made it. I never kept up with what he spent — it didn't matter because it was his money and he always had enough left over to buy me a nice gift and get us back home.

"One day, I told him I'd like to go somewhere different for a change, like Canada. I just wanted to go some place I had never been.

"He sulked for a week until I gave up and said, 'Fine, we'll go wherever you want to.' We ended up in Atlantic City, and for the first time, I got bored — maybe more of a mixture of anger and boredom.

"If you're not a gambler yourself, sitting at those tables night after night, smelling cigarette smoke and watching waitresses bring drink after drink gets stifling.

"When we got to Atlantic City the first night, I started flirting with this cute blond guy at the next table, just to make Kirk jealous.

"Even though I was talking to another man, Kirk didn't seem to notice for the longest time. That made me madder by the minute.

"Finally, Kirk seemed so oblivious to me, I decided I didn't give a damn. I excused myself and went to talk to the other guy. Kirk didn't even flinch. After I started talking to this guy, I told him I'd been wanting to go to this piano bar down on the wharf. He said he wasn't doing so hot at blackjack and would be glad to walk down there and have a drink.

"I said, 'Let's go,' loud enough for the whole casino to hear. Then I made a point of walking out with him, laughing, so there was no way Kirk could help but notice.

"This guy and I went down to the bar and had a great time, laughing and listening to the piano player. It was okay, but I kept checking my watch every five minutes. I was determined to stay out late, at least late enough to be fairly certain that Kirk was back in the room.

"When I finally went back to our room, he was there. I really didn't know whether to expect an argument or the silent treatment. It turned out to be the latter.

"I had never seen him so quiet. I walked in and ignored him, without so much as a 'Hello.' When I looked at him, I really thought he was going to cry. He was totally out of character.

"Before I could utter a word, he told me that he loved me and that he didn't want me to leave him. I told him I was tired of the gambling, and of everything else, like his always deciding when and where we went all the time. He didn't say anything else, so I washed my face, climbed into the other double bed and went to sleep."

HOW TO HANDLE THIS MAN

Risk takers, as slightly off the beaten path as they may be, rarely say they love you if they are not absolutely sure they mean it. The problem is trying to find a common ground between his risk taking and his love.

This kind of man needs a special woman, one who can be part lover and part governess. He needs a woman who knows how to keep up with him in every way.

Inside, the need to gamble or take a gamble at life comes from a need to feel in control of something, since they know they cannot control life. True gamblers need professional help if they are to step outside the casino for good. The vast majority of risk takers simply need a strong woman who loves them for what they are: exciting men tackling life the only way they know how.

Denise was in the middle of her struggle to find that ground when we first spoke. She was not sure which way to turn, so she broke off the relationship for several months before we talked again. When she did call, she sounded much more like a woman at ease with herself and with her life than the young woman she had been before.

She explained that after a great deal of soul-searching, she had come to the decision that she wanted to give the relationship with Kirk one more try, but this time on more solid ground.

Denise explained that the first night she called him back, they stayed up all night talking about everything, particularly parts of his past he had never mentioned before. She learned that Kirk was fourteen when he and his then twelve-year-old sister were orphaned. He had dropped out of high school and worked to help support them and their aging grandmother. The day he turned eighteen, he joined the Army and had helped his sister finish high school and then put her through college.

"I felt like I really knew him for the first time," Denise says. "After hearing where he had come from, I began to understand why he is the way he is today.

"Because he had discovered early that working regular jobs to get ahead is a tough, day-to-day struggle, he had learned to take risks in an attempt to find shortcuts or some pot of gold at the end of the rainbow. For the first time, I had a very tender, almost motherly, affection towards him.

"Now, we've been back together almost two months, and it feels like it may last, but I'm still a long way from making a long-term commitment.

"The good part now, though, is that I know

where to set the limits. I've told him that if he ever puts his gambling before our relationship, I will walk out of his life, period. That doesn't mean I want him to follow me around like a puppy dog or give up ever taking risks, because his ability to take risks is a big part of why I love him.

"It was the hard-core gambling that really got me.

"Things are much better now. We make decisions together. We plan our days and nights together. And we're having a great time.

"If I had to say why I think it's working now is simple. I know where he is coming from and he knows where I am coming from. We give and take. He's not a total taker anymore."

Denise adds that even Kirk was taken by the Canadian countryside on their recent trip.

MAN HANDLING TIPS

1. Use an invisible net.

2. Make him accountable for his actions.

3. Make sure *you* roll the dice.

CHAPTER XV

Mr. Save-The Snails

Traits: Bookish
              Passionate
              Persistent

Likes: Underdogs
              Nature
              Low-Fat Foods

Dislikes: Pollution
              Big Business
              Congress

His Ideal Woman: Wholesome
                       Visionary
                       Committed

HIS PROFILE

Johnny Appleseed had nothing on this man.

His whole life is consumed with saving the world, from the bees and trees to the whales and snails.

How did he get this way? It could have been anything from having a nature loving mother to having brushed shoulders with big business long enough to know the dollar usually rules the world, people and animals and the environment be damned.

What does it take to keep up with this kind of man? One of two things — either a common belief in saving the world or a deep respect for his ideals that is strong enough to help him wage his war of peace.

JODI'S STORY

"I met him when he first moved to town and came in to open an account," says Jodi, 23, a bank teller in Colorado Springs. "Trey seemed so innocent even though he was seven years older than I was.

"He had straggly long hair and was wearing a 'Save the Earth' T-shirt, jeans and sandals. The minute I saw him, I knew he probably drove an old Volkswagen with a Greenpeace bumper sticker.

"He would come into the bank once or twice a week. He was very nice, and I noticed that he always came to my line whenever he came in.

"One day, he gave me the deposit, and as I handed him back his slip and asked if there was anything else I could do for him, he stammered and said, 'Yes. Would you have lunch with me one day?'

"I was surprised but said I would. I told him my next day off, and he said he would meet me in front of the bank. When I pulled up, he was leaning up against his car, an old Oldsmobile, not a VW. There were a lot of 'Save This' and 'Save That' bumpers stickers, just as I had suspected.

"I smiled to myself thinking that I was at least half right.

"He told me he had made a picnic lunch that we could take down to the river. Seeing his car, I asked him if he'd like to ride with me. He reached into the back seat and pulled out a big wicker picnic basket.

"It was a beautiful day, and since it was in the middle of the week, the lake was practically deserted.

"Trey was so cute. He spread a red and

white checkered tablecloth on the ground, then started laying out the food. It was a feast, but different than what I was used to. Instead of paper plates and plastic forks, it was real dishes and silverware. Instead of fried chicken and potato salad, it was veggie pitas and different kinds of fruit.

"It was delicious, and the afternoon was perfect. We talked, or rather, Trey talked for hours, about everything from the environment to pollution to what he as an individual and we as human beings could do, not what we had to do, to stop what he saw as the annihilation of the planet.

"I was entranced. The biggest environmental concern I had was whether or not my car would pass the emissions test. Trey opened up a whole new world, no pun intended, talking about what he saw as his destiny or reason for living and that was, as trite as it may sound, to the save the earth."

Jodi says that as they began to see more and more of one another, she realized that while she whole-heartedly supported his position and beliefs, she would never be as absorbed in the cause as Trey.

It was not that she did not care. She did. But she also cared about things which did not seem to concern him, like getting ahead in life far enough to build a secure financial future.

"We've been together now about eight months," Jodi says. "I've tried to tell him what kind of future I've been looking forward to, and he does understand, at least as much as I understand his dreams.

"At this point, we're both young enough to let things happen and see how it goes.

"In the meantime, I am thankful I got to know him. There is something special about a man who truly cares more about other people and other things than himself."

Susan Thomas

HOW TO HANDLE THIS MAN

Tenderness. That is the only way a woman will ever make room in this man's heart for her because his heart is already packed with compassion and love for life and all of its creatures.

A woman who considers hooking up with this kind of man will be doing both of them an important favor if she takes him for what he is and harbors no illusions of changing him.

That, simply, is impossible.

Still, a woman who does not naturally possess his passion for crusading does not necessarily have to count herself out if she falls for this man. He needs the love and support of a woman who believes in him, as much or more than his cause.

There are differences in even the strongest relationship, and it is often these differences which generate the solidity.

If you can take this man along with his dreams, you may have a hand in saving the world without doing anything but being in love. But be warned.

For if you are a woman digging for gold, you will find yourself sinking in fool's gold if you ever expect this man to put money in sports cars, classy condominiums or country club dues.

It is not going to happen.

MAN HANDLING TIPS

1. Love animals.

2. Have some dreams of your own.

3. Learn to eat tofu.

CHAPTER XVI

Mr. Not-In-This-Lifetime

Traits: Clever
Insecure
Underlying Anger

Likes: Control
Perfection
Dominance

Dislikes: Themselves
Successful Men
Successful Women

His Ideal Woman: Submissive
Insecure
Quiet

HIS PROFILE

If there is one type of man this world could do without, this is the one. To his credit, it is not always his fault. Usually, this man was either abused as a child, or for whatever reasons, never developed the social skills to integrate into the mainstream. He was the kid on the playground who was last to be picked for the kickball team. Once grown, he can never have meaningful relationships with anyone, most importantly, himself.

Beware! This man can be extremely tricky. Because of a gaping hole in his emotional composition, he develops clever ways to hide his anger. He can be charming, handsome — even funny on occasion. He will never have trouble finding a women, but can rarely keep a good one for long because his charm is truly only skin-deep. That's why he preys upon the nicest women among us — those who share insecurities which can be preyed upon by these spineless vultures.

MARIE'S STORY

"It was so sudden, as if something went 'click,'" says Marie, 31, a Manhattan graphic artist.

"He was great. Then he turned into a monster."

It was her fifth date with Rick.

"Up until that moment, I thought I might have finally found my dream man," Marie says. "We'd met through co-workers — not at a bar — and Rick seemed to have everything. He was good looking, had a Masters Degree in math and had been the perfect gentleman on our first four dates.

"That night, I was so excited before we went out because we'd planned the perfect evening — drinks, dinner, dancing and then home to my place for a night-cap.

"Beyond kisses and a few caresses, it had been all romance up till then — no sex — but it seemed right that night. I made sure to wear my lacy lingerie and sexiest red dress.

"Until we got into the elevator to my loft, it was a perfect evening.

"Over drinks, he told a hilarious string of jokes that made me laugh so hard my mascara started running, and dinner was romantically fabulous. Then we went to this great after-hours dance club.

"I felt like I was sixteen again dancing with him to 'When A Man Loves A Woman.' It was almost too good to be true. We couldn't have had a better time; everything seemed so perfect.

"But, looking back, it went from wonderful

to crazy in a split second.

"When we returned to my building, we got into the elevator with another guy, a nice-looking young man I had never seen before.

"The elevator was one of those old cage elevators, and I was standing a little too close to the edge when the young guy pulled the metal gate down and accidently grazed the heel of my shoe.

"I let out a little laugh, smiling at the guy because it was my fault for standing too close.

"But then I heard Rick saying something like, 'Don't you think you owe this lady an apology?'

"I looked at this young guy, he looked at me, and we were both puzzled.

"I tried to laugh again, saying something like, 'It's okay, no problem.'

"But Rick repeated the question gruffly, as if I didn't exist.

"Finally, the other guy, shaking his head, muttered an apology.

"When Rick and I walked in my loft, I stopped inside the kitchen. All I said was, 'Why did you do that? It was my fault.'

"That's when it happened. He flew into a rage.

"It was so quick, I don't remember what he said. All I remember is that his face got so red and distorted, I hardly recognized him.

"He started yelling, something about respecting women. It really didn't make much sense.

"With my big mouth, I started shouting back.

"Before I knew it, he reached out and pushed me, hard.

"I fell backwards against the counter top, scraping my backbone as I slid to the floor.

"I remember my bottom hitting the floor

with a hard thud, then everything stopped.

"In an instant, Rick was the old Rick again, leaning over me, saying he was sorry, and trying to help me up.

"I burst out crying, shook up and confused by the whole episode.

"He said he was sorry, over and over again, as I sat there squalling.

"Then, thank God, my senses came back.

"Pushing his outstretched arms away from me, I stood up, straightened my wrinkled red dress and wiped my face with a paper towel.

"Then I told him to get out."

When he protested, Marie picked up the telephone and dialed 911.

Rick left.

"It was one the smartest things I've ever done in my life," Marie says, looking back.

"Now, I've found a new boyfriend who would cut off his hand before he ever shoved me or hit me.

"Believe it or not, Rick had the nerve to call me for weeks after that night trying to tell me how sorry he was and that it would never happen again.

"I let him talk to my answering machine."

HOW TO HANDLE THIS MAN

Although she does not consider herself a particularly brave woman, Marie showed tremendous courage that night.

Any man who is physically, sexually, or emotionally abusive — from a push or shove to derogatory comments or worse — is *poison*. The fact is tragically proven every hour of every day as women across the country are battered or murdered by husbands or lovers who profess love for their victims.

Don't become another statistic.

Don't wait for it to happen again.

Don't listen to the "I'm so sorry" the first time. Excuses for violent behavior — from "I drank too much" to "I was upset over work" — are ridiculous.

There is *nothing* to excuse physical violence or emotional abuse.

Men who feel the need to physically hurt a woman or insult her have something wrong with them — something only professionals can fix — and that is only if the man is fortunate.

Whenever you meet a new man, look for the early warning signs. Do not forget that battering men prey on the weakest of women, those with low self-esteem who are looking for acceptance. Be strong. No matter what line this clever animal may offer, no woman deserves to be abused.

Call a friend, call the police, or just run.
And never look back.

MAN HANDLING TIPS

1. Smell this rat as soon as possible.

2. Never be embarrassed by the first act of abuse. *You* are the victim.

3. Get up, get out, and get help.

CHAPTER XVII

Mr. Dream-A-Little-Dream-With-Me

Traits: Optimistic
Playful
Futuristic

Likes: Adventure
Solitude
Loyalty

Dislikes: Regimentation
Planning
Deadlines

His Ideal Woman: Intelligent
Trusting
Flexible

HIS PROFILE

He is adorable. This man-boy can daydream you into his dreams like a hypnotist. His words are magical, lulling the smartest woman back to the days when she believed in Cinderella. The world is his, in every aspect, because no matter what hand is dealt him, he can turn it into an adventure. The fact is, he is completely taken by life. Every atom entices him. He is on earth to take in as much as he can during his time here.

No doubt both of his parents were intelligent. They passed those genes on to him along with an internal drive to go on searching for the best place to be and the best thing to be doing at any given time. This devil-may-care attitude makes him the hit at parties because he truly refuses to live life by the rules, a trait many people would kill for but can never quite grasp. He is gentle, wrapping every moment with love.

JANE'S STORY

"He was young, eager and great in bed," says Jane, 30, a real estate agent in Dallas.

"What more could I ask for?"

Tim, then living in Vermont, was, she says, like a fast-action hero.

Unlike her rigid schedule and organized life, falling in love with Tim was like riding a tornado. Everything was spur of the moment. A date for dinner turned into a weekend trampling through the mountains. A Saturday morning kiss turned into an all-day love in, with breakfast, lunch and dinner in bed. A concert brought first-row seats after Tim called ahead and used his charm to mention he was with the entertainer's entourage. Everything was fun, vibrant, and alive.

Their love affair was well into its first year before an alarm began sounding in Jane's head. Something was not right.

"He was educated, with a master's degree and a list of accomplished jobs," she says. "He had been an administrative aide to an influential Congressman in Washington. He had worked at a prestigious public relations firm in New York, and was teaching at a very expensive prep school for boys in Vermont when we met.

"I was living in Texas at the time, so the long-distance relationship made the time we spent together rather magical.

"Just before Christmas he called and said he had decided to take a sabbatical from school because he wanted to try his hand at writing. He said he could write anywhere, so he decided to move to Texas to be closer to me.

"I was thrilled at first and for a couple of months, everything was perfect. We had separate apartments, but a day never passed that we weren't together at his place or mine. To my amazement, the magic of the long-distance relationship failed to disappear. It was a great as ever.

"Soon, little things began popping up.

"First, his car broke down, so we started sharing mine. It wasn't that much of an inconvenience because he would drop me off and pick me up wherever I needed to go. A couple of weeks later, I stopped asking when his car would be fixed.

"Then, there was an expensive civic dinner which I really wanted to attend because I knew I could meet a lot of people who would be great to get to know in my business. When I told Tim about it, he bashfully admitted he didn't have the one hundred dollar-a-plate to spare, so I told him it was my treat. We went, and like always, everyone looked at us saying we were the perfect couple.

"As the months passed, I paid for nearly everything we did. I tried to keep telling myself that I was a wonderful, liberated woman, and that he would repay me as soon as he could get some of his writing published.

"It wasn't until about six months later when I realized that he hadn't written the first sentence. Not even the first word.

"I had had the work ethic driven into me with a jackhammer by my parents, and that burned me up. He hadn't been doing *anything* toward his writing dream. When I confronted Tim, he became very defensive and said he hadn't found the proper 'inspiration' yet.

"I didn't understand where he was coming from, and it went on like that for a while.

"Finally, I realized what it was. He was a gypsy, through and through. Even though he was intelligent and had the education to do anything he wanted, he would never settle down at one job and stick with it. More importantly to me, he would never be an equal provider in a marriage.

"I want things like children and stability. I want to be equals, not the one who has to make sure all the bills are paid.

"I love him desperately, but it's a hard choice I'm going to have to make.

"Do I want Tim and adventure, or someone else and security?"

HOW TO HANDLE THIS MAN

Jane, like most women who fall in love with dreamers, eventually found herself at a painful crossroads, with her heart pointing in one direction and her head in another.

Should a woman exchange her dreams of a stable future for the love of a man who will always be part boy? It is a tough call, one that very much depends on the woman you are.

A few women are perfect matches for this type of man. They are women who are dreamers themselves, caring more about trekking through the woods in a spring rain than about diamonds. These are women who usually hold down professional jobs, from museum curators to small business owners. They are secure within themselves, knowing that they alone can support themselves and their dreamer, without one fleeting regret.

However, the vast majority of women do not fall into that category. Most women, through no fault of their own, are trapped by the visions which were burned into them since childhood — the man should be the primary, or at least equal, provider.

Because that ideal is instilled in so many women, handling a dreamer is difficult because the answer lies within the woman. First and foremost, you must decide which kind of woman you are. Then, you have to fully realize that this man will never change, no matter what you say or do. Adventure is in his soul.

At that point, have a frank discussion with yourself.

As the years pass, will you be able to run off with him and the children when he decides to go digging for ancient Mayan ruins? Will you resent never owning a big home and a large stock portfolio? Can you throw away your yearning for the white picket fence?

Love is not at question here. You cannot help but love him. But can you be happy being the primary provider for a man who, while he will cherish you from head to toe, will never stay in one place or one job long enough to grow roots?

The answer lies within you, alone.

The pressure is on you to make a fair decision for both of you. If you cannot be absolutely sure you can relinquish your dreams of a more conventional lifestyle, leave him while you are still in love. If you lie to yourself now, chances are you will become a nagging wife and he will leave you flat.

Jane made the decision that she could not conform to a life of nonconformity. She and Tim parted as friends. She later married a doctor and is now happy, secure, and expecting her second child.

Since her peaceful break-up with Tim, she says she has come to grips with two things.

"I made the right decision," she says, "but a little part of me will always love him, following him wherever his adventures lead him."

Susan Thomas

MAN HANDLING TIPS

1. Listen to his dreams

2. Know, with certainty, he will be the same until the day he dies.

3. Realize you can love him and still let him go.

CHAPTER XVIII

Mr. Take-Two

Traits: Intelligent
Extroverted
Egotist

Likes: Praise
Politics
Material Possessions

Dislikes: Higher Authority
Opposing Viewpoints
Lack of Ambition

His Ideal Woman: Classy
Wealthy
Subservient

HIS PROFILE

When it comes to what women of past generations once called "a great catch," this was their man. Intelligent. Educated. Going Places. The difference today is that more and more women are also educated and going places, too.

That makes for a new ballgame for this man who once ruled the world. Though the playing field of today still leans his way, it has become tilted enough that this man no longer feels as at ease as he once did. That uneasiness seems to have brought out the worst in him.

Many of these men feel even more compelled to fight for the spotlight, and too often, leave their love interests in the wings as the men run center stage.

This is not to say that all these men are self-centered or worthless. There are some good ones left. If you happen to be a woman looking for a meaningful relationship and you bump shoulders with one of these new up-and-comers, beware.

They are as cagy as men get.

ABIGAIL'S STORY

"Picture this," says Abigail, 29, a magazine editor from Omaha.

"I was invited to a dinner party at my best friend's house. A woman who was supposed to be the dinner guest of a famous doctor from London had been forced to cancel at the last minute. She was desperate to find a date for him, so I agreed to help her out.

"I left my office at seven, thinking I'd miss most of the rush hour traffic in Dallas on a Friday night. Wrong. I barely made it to my condo in time to splash water on my face, throw on a decent dress and run a couple of redlights to get to my friend's house by eight.

"As I pulled into the driveway behind a Mercedes, I threw open the door and, as I'm pulling the key out of the ignition, BAM!

"I'd forgotten to put it into park, so my car lunged forward the moment my foot slid off the brake pedal, crashing into the Mercedes. At the same time, my head slammed into my windshield.

"All I remember is being carried inside with my head pounding horribly, and a distinctively British voice calming me down.

"That was my introduction to David."

At 29, Abigail had worked her way up the ladder to art editor of a national scientific magazine. Having never lacked for a love interest, she was happily consumed with her career and wasn't looking for marriage.

"David was different," she says. "Maybe every woman says that when she meets someone she really cares about, but it was no exaggeration. Beyond being a surgeon, something that completely fascinated me, David was also very committed to helping his country find some civilized way to stop the bloodshed between the Catholics and the Protestants.

"I was taken. Totally."

Lovemaking, she says, "was like having a man with the softest and most skilled lips, hands and body make the perfect moves at the perfect times, every time."

Within months, Abigail says she was absorbed into David's trans-Atlantic world.

"I kept my job, but when we weren't together, my thoughts were always with him," she says, "either remembering our last time together or thinking of the social efforts to stop the crazy bombings in London and Dublin."

Her connections to the American media didn't hurt. On one trip to the British Isles, she took along her camera and compiled an "American Eye" piece on the war in Northern Ireland which was warmly received by both David and her magazine's American readers.

"I truly cared about the war, not just because of David, but I would never have gotten that involved without him," she says. "That's why I was stunned the night it happened."

The evening of which she speaks occurred almost a year into Abigail and David's relationship. They were in London to attend a dinner for the political peacemakers in Northern Ireland. She knew a close friend of David's was hosting a small get-together after the dinner in the penthouse of the hotel with the officials.

She did not have an inkling that David would exclude her.

"I'll never forget his words," she says. "He said, 'Listen love, do come along back to my flat after the reception.' It was like he was saying, 'Run along now, little American girl, until we get close enough to my bed.'

"I cannot deny that it hurt me very badly. I walked out of the hotel in a daze, caught a taxi to his apartment, grabbed my things and checked into a hotel. I ordered a bottle of wine and cried. I am still not sure whether I felt used, abused or just mad as hell because he apparently thought he could use me, and my mind, when he wanted to, then send me off to his bed to await his arrival when he wanted center stage at the reception.

"The next morning, I caught the first flight back to the states. That was six months ago. He has called me non-stop since then, but I've never felt the same."

HOW TO HANDLE THIS MAN

The good news for Abigail and the bad news for David is that in their relationship, he blew it. She cared about him. She became involved not only with a man, but also his concerns and dreams. He slammed the door in her face, obviously assuming his "command" of their relationship would rule.

Today, Abigail says David continued to call for almost two years, at the end pleading for her to explain why she left so abruptly.

"I knew if I had to explain to him why I felt so hurt, he wouldn't understand it," she says. "All I can do is thank my lucky stars for having a family who taught me during my formative years that loving takes more than words. Actions can speak *volumes*.

"I now have friends who are married to these types of men who literally use them to make themselves look good, with no concern about how the women feel. It's really sad."

There is a middle ground between Abigail's reflex shutoff valve with David and her friends' current lifestyle with these types of men.

The key is to recognize that while these men have lives that involve more than their love for a woman, the woman must always make it crystal clear that she will love and support him — but never become a stepladder.

They will be partners, or they will not be together. There will be give and take, but he must not take more than his share. If there is a public spotlight for their joint efforts, they must share it, together.

MAN HANDLING TIPS

1. Your life is as important as his.

2. Act like a doormat and you will be stepped on.

3. Keep an escape plan for those times his head begins to swell.